SAMSON
JUDGE OF ISRAEL

METRON PRESS™

SAMSON: Judge of Israel
Adapted from the *Contemporary English Version* of the Bible.

Samson: Copyright © 2002, American Bible Society. All Rights Reserved.

ISBN 1-58516 - 647 - 2

Printed in the United States of America
Eng. Comic - Samson - 112657
ABS - 11/02 - 25,000 —MW1
Metron Press is an imprint of the American Bible Society.

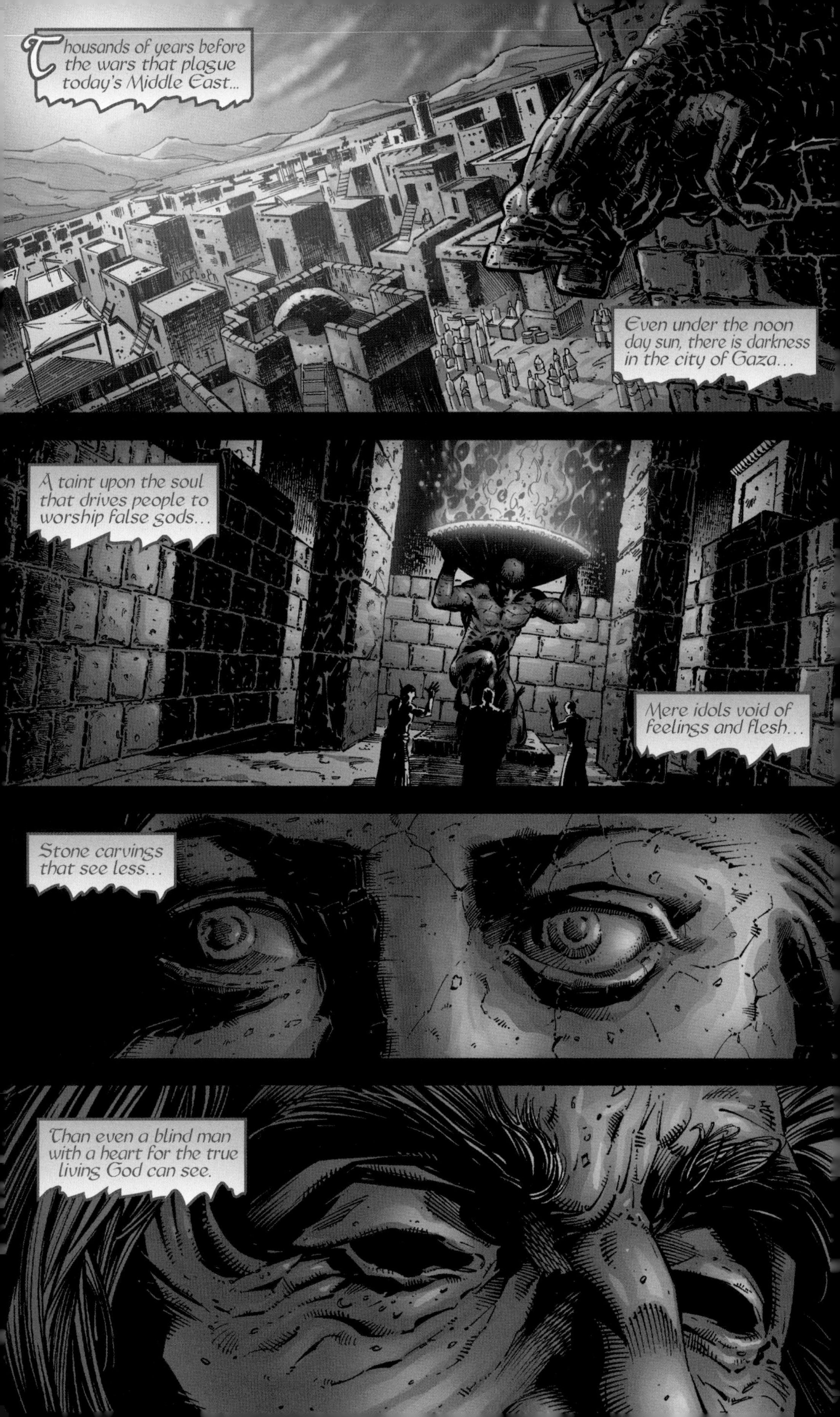
Thousands of years before the wars that plague today's Middle East...
Even under the noon day sun, there is darkness in the city of Gaza...
A taint upon the soul that drives people to worship false gods...
Mere idols void of feelings and flesh...
Stone carvings that see less...
Than even a blind man with a heart for the true living God can see.

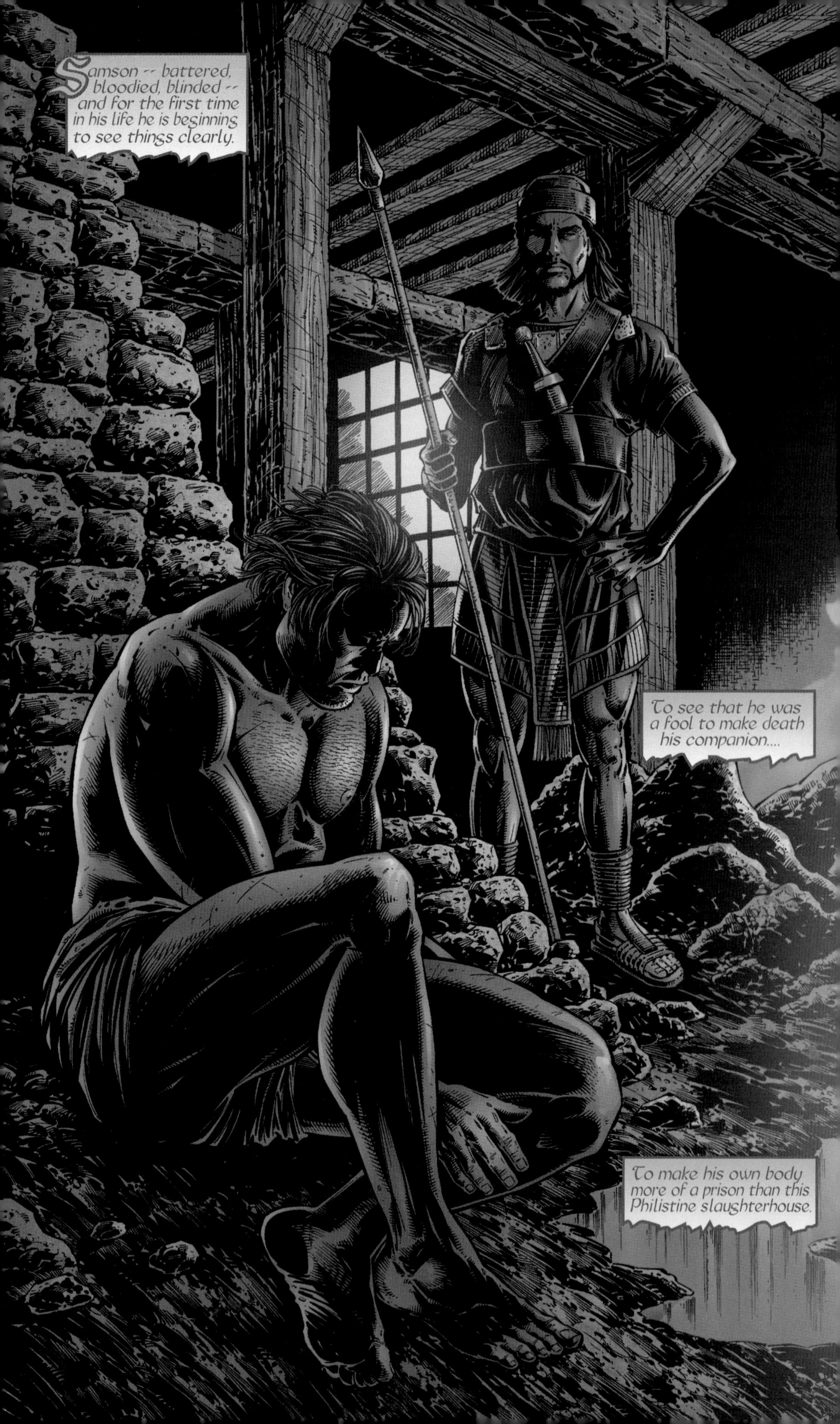
Samson -- battered, bloodied, blinded -- and for the first time in his life he is beginning to see things clearly.
To see that he was a fool to make death his companion....
To make his own body more of a prison than this Philistine slaughterhouse.

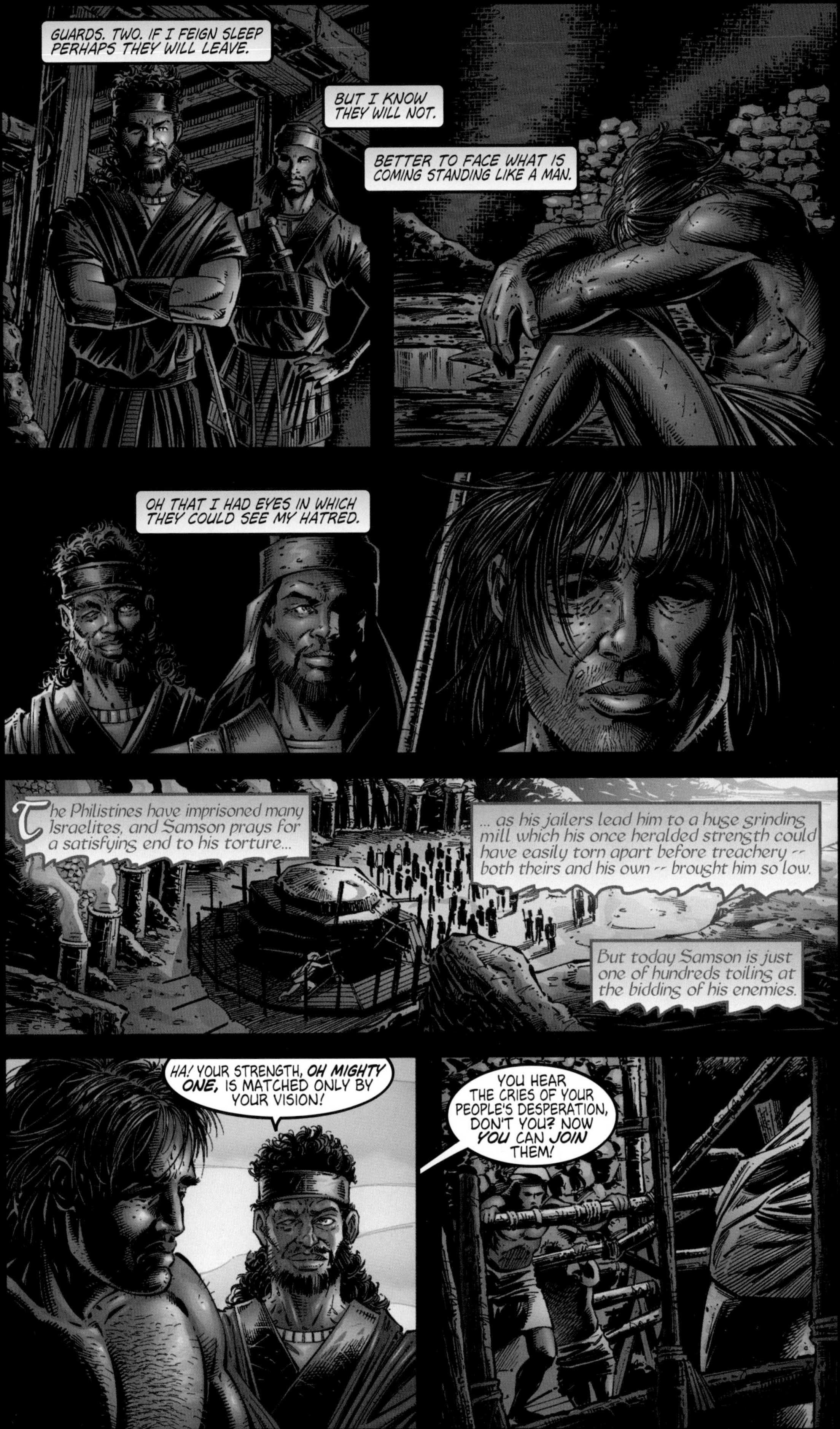
GUARDS. TWO. IF I FEIGN SLEEP PERHAPS THEY WILL LEAVE.
BUT I KNOW THEY WILL NOT.
BETTER TO FACE WHAT IS COMING STANDING LIKE A MAN.
OH THAT I HAD EYES IN WHICH THEY COULD SEE MY HATRED.
The Philistines have imprisoned many Israelites, and Samson prays for a satisfying end to his torture...
... as his jailers lead him to a huge grinding mill which his once heralded strength could have easily torn apart before treachery -- both theirs and his own -- brought him so low.
But today Samson is just one of hundreds toiling at the bidding of his enemies.
HA! YOUR STRENGTH, OH MIGHTY ONE, IS MATCHED ONLY BY YOUR VISION!
YOU HEAR THE CRIES OF YOUR PEOPLE'S DESPERATION, DON'T YOU? NOW YOU CAN JOIN THEM!

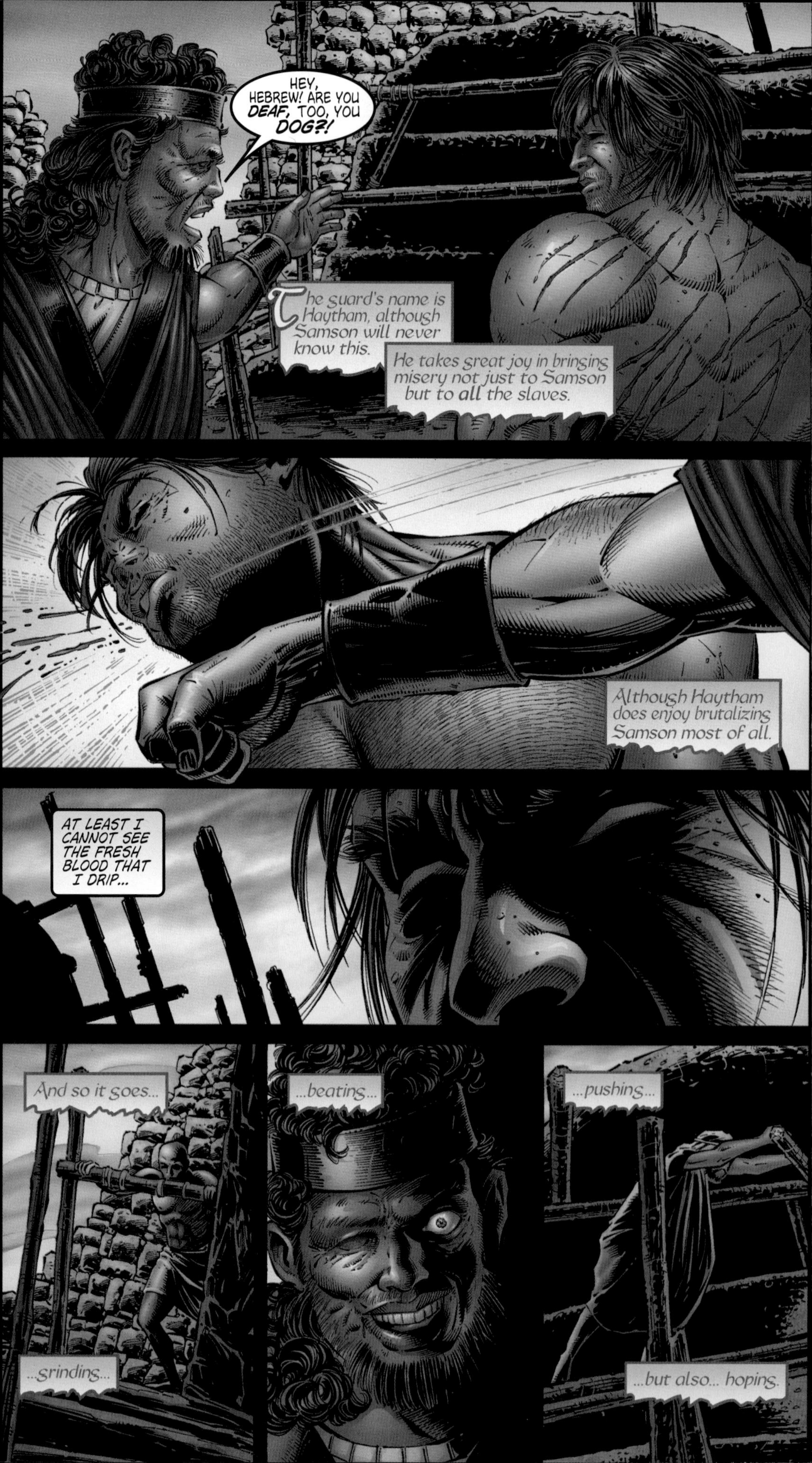
HEY, HEBREW! ARE YOU DEAF, TOO, YOU DOG?!
The guard's name is Haytham, although Samson will never know this.
He takes great joy in bringing misery not just to Samson but to all the slaves.
Although Haytham does enjoy brutalizing Samson most of all.
AT LEAST I CANNOT SEE THE FRESH BLOOD THAT I DRIP...
And so it goes...
...grinding...
...beating...
...pushing...
...but also... hoping.

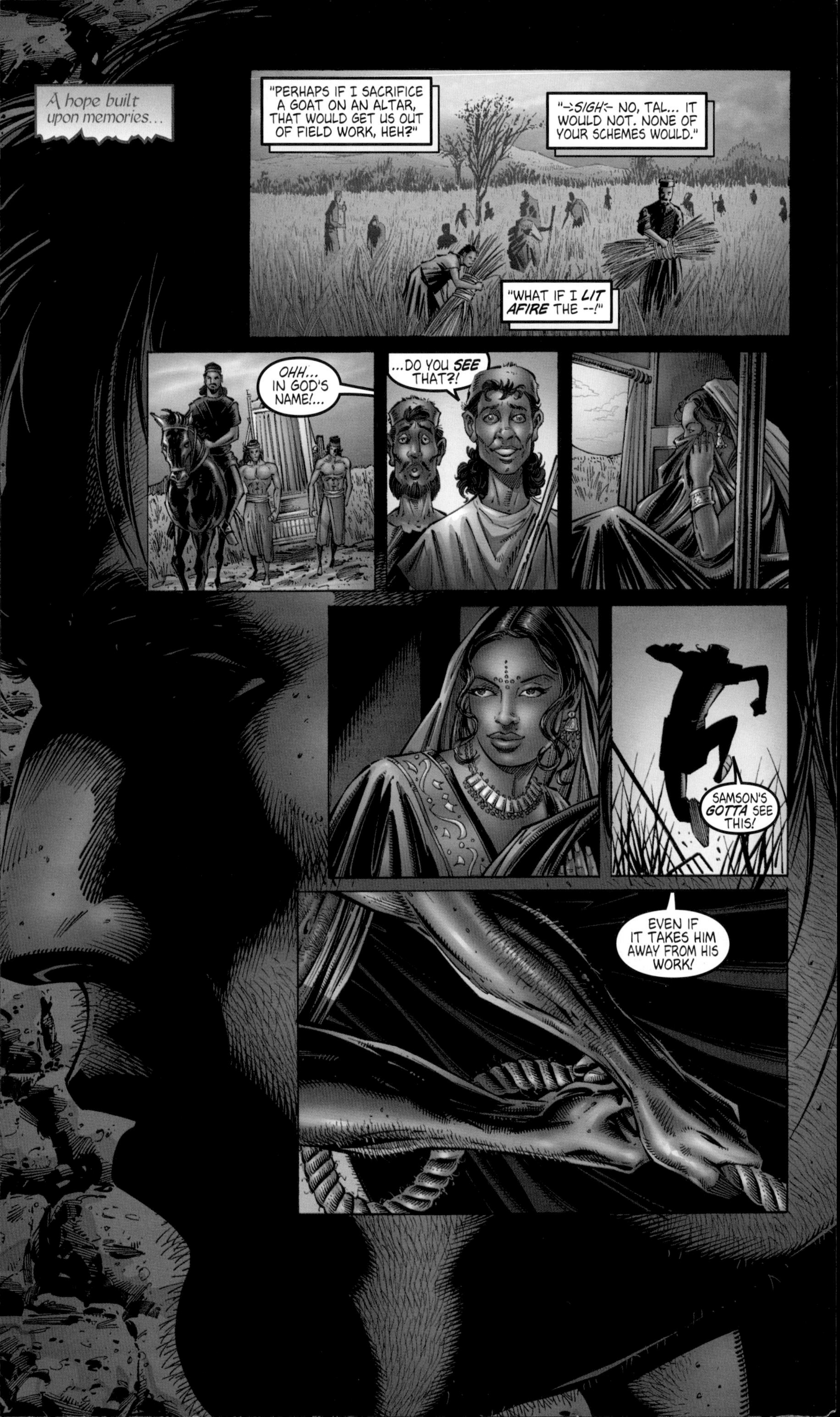
A hope built upon memories...
"PERHAPS IF I SACRIFICE A GOAT ON AN ALTAR, THAT WOULD GET US OUT OF FIELD WORK, HEH?"
"-SIGH- NO, TAL... IT WOULD NOT. NONE OF YOUR SCHEMES WOULD."
"WHAT IF I LIT AFIRE THE --!"
OHH... IN GOD'S NAME!...
...DO YOU SEE THAT?!
SAMSON'S GOTTA SEE THIS!
EVEN IF IT TAKES HIM AWAY FROM HIS WORK!

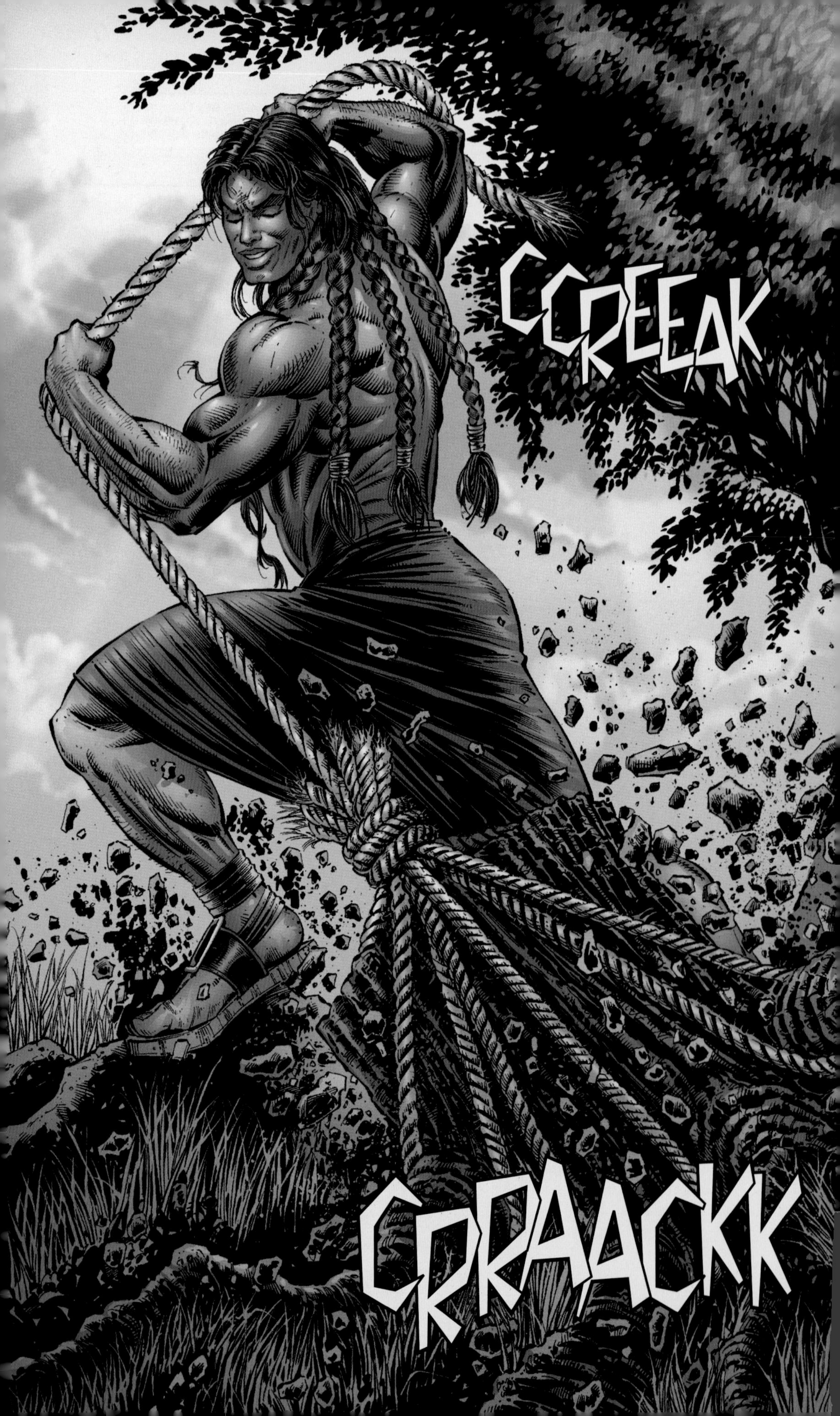
CCREEAK
CRRAACKK

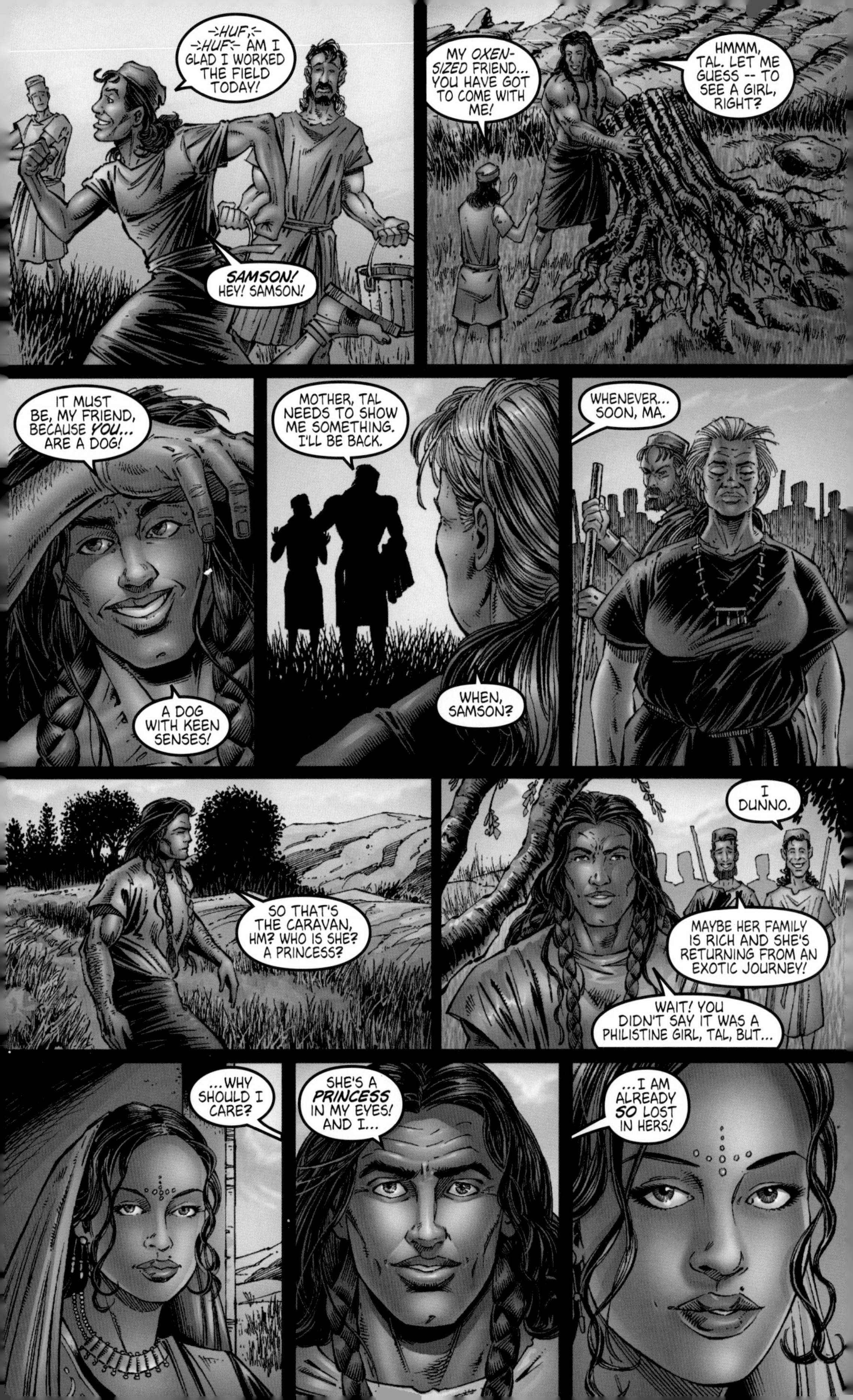

-HUF- -HUF- AM I GLAD I WORKED THE FIELD TODAY!
SAMSON! HEY! SAMSON!
MY OXEN-SIZED FRIEND... YOU HAVE GOT TO COME WITH ME!
HMMM, TAL. LET ME GUESS -- TO SEE A GIRL, RIGHT?
IT MUST BE, MY FRIEND, BECAUSE YOU... ARE A DOG!
A DOG WITH KEEN SENSES!
MOTHER, TAL NEEDS TO SHOW ME SOMETHING. I'LL BE BACK.
WHEN, SAMSON?
WHENEVER... SOON, MA.
SO THAT'S THE CARAVAN, HM? WHO IS SHE? A PRINCESS?
I DUNNO.
MAYBE HER FAMILY IS RICH AND SHE'S RETURNING FROM AN EXOTIC JOURNEY!
WAIT! YOU DIDN'T SAY IT WAS A PHILISTINE GIRL, TAL, BUT...
...WHY SHOULD I CARE?
SHE'S A PRINCESS IN MY EYES! AND I...
...I AM ALREADY SO LOST IN HERS!

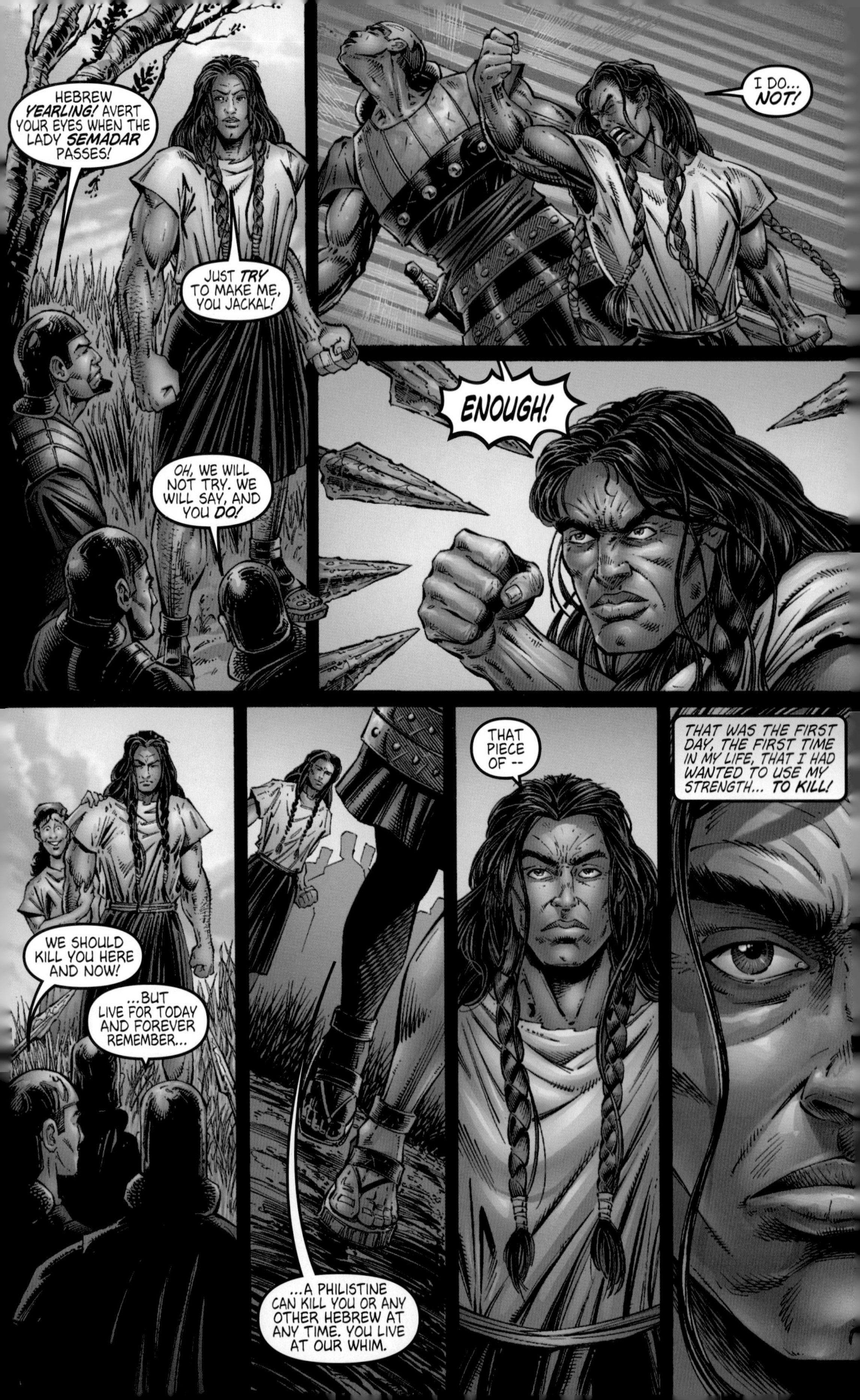
HEBREW YEARLING! AVERT YOUR EYES WHEN THE LADY SEMADAR PASSES!
JUST TRY TO MAKE ME, YOU JACKAL!
OH, WE WILL NOT TRY. WE WILL SAY, AND YOU DO!
I DO... NOT!
ENOUGH!
WE SHOULD KILL YOU HERE AND NOW!
...BUT LIVE FOR TODAY AND FOREVER REMEMBER...
...A PHILISTINE CAN KILL YOU OR ANY OTHER HEBREW AT ANY TIME. YOU LIVE AT OUR WHIM.
THAT PIECE OF --
THAT WAS THE FIRST DAY, THE FIRST TIME IN MY LIFE, THAT I HAD WANTED TO USE MY STRENGTH... TO KILL!

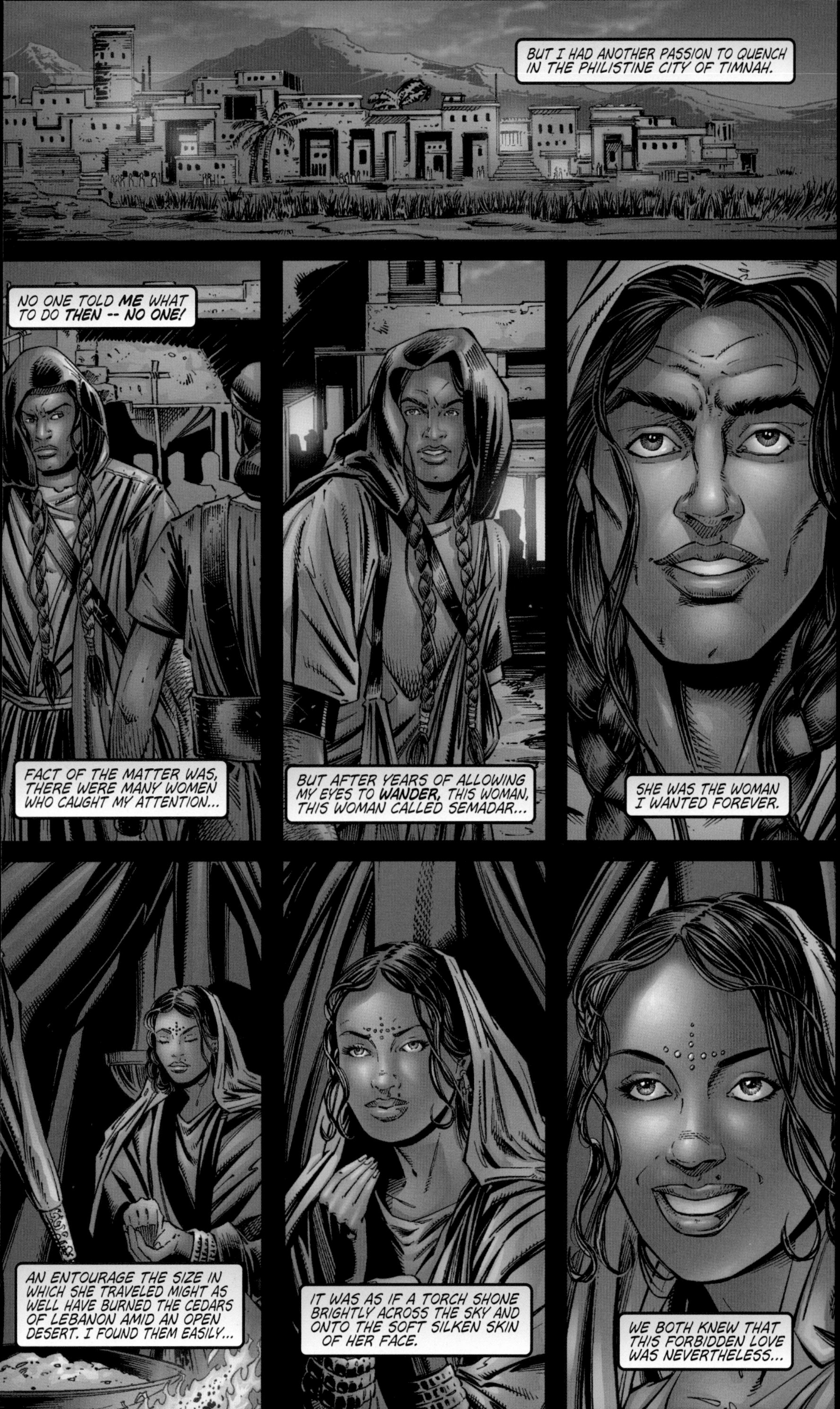
BUT I HAD ANOTHER PASSION TO QUENCH IN THE PHILISTINE CITY OF TIMNAH.
NO ONE TOLD **ME** WHAT TO DO **THEN** -- **NO ONE!**
FACT OF THE MATTER WAS, THERE WERE MANY WOMEN WHO CAUGHT MY ATTENTION...
BUT AFTER YEARS OF ALLOWING MY EYES TO **WANDER,** THIS WOMAN, THIS WOMAN CALLED SEMADAR...
SHE WAS THE WOMAN I WANTED FOREVER.
AN ENTOURAGE THE SIZE IN WHICH SHE TRAVELED MIGHT AS WELL HAVE BURNED THE CEDARS OF LEBANON AMID AN OPEN DESERT. I FOUND THEM EASILY...
IT WAS AS IF A TORCH SHONE BRIGHTLY ACROSS THE SKY AND ONTO THE SOFT SILKEN SKIN OF HER FACE.
WE BOTH KNEW THAT THIS FORBIDDEN LOVE WAS NEVERTHELESS...

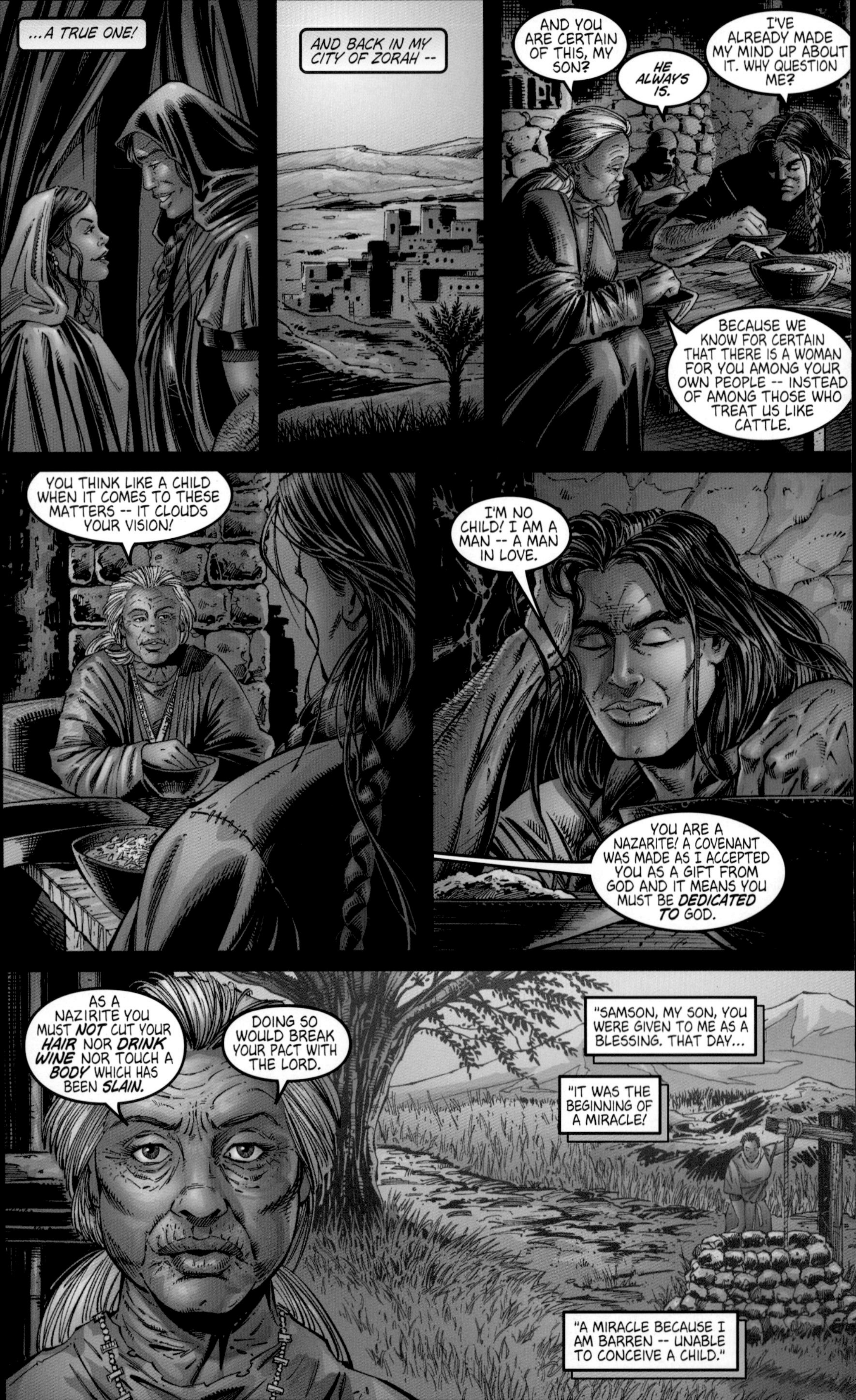
...A TRUE ONE!
AND BACK IN MY CITY OF ZORAH --
AND YOU ARE CERTAIN OF THIS, MY SON?
HE ALWAYS IS.
I'VE ALREADY MADE MY MIND UP ABOUT IT. WHY QUESTION ME?
BECAUSE WE KNOW FOR CERTAIN THAT THERE IS A WOMAN FOR YOU AMONG YOUR OWN PEOPLE -- INSTEAD OF AMONG THOSE WHO TREAT US LIKE CATTLE.
YOU THINK LIKE A CHILD WHEN IT COMES TO THESE MATTERS -- IT CLOUDS YOUR VISION!
I'M NO CHILD! I AM A MAN -- A MAN IN LOVE.
YOU ARE A NAZARITE! A COVENANT WAS MADE AS I ACCEPTED YOU AS A GIFT FROM GOD AND IT MEANS YOU MUST BE DEDICATED TO GOD.
AS A NAZIRITE YOU MUST NOT CUT YOUR HAIR NOR DRINK WINE NOR TOUCH A BODY WHICH HAS BEEN SLAIN.
DOING SO WOULD BREAK YOUR PACT WITH THE LORD.
"SAMSON, MY SON, YOU WERE GIVEN TO ME AS A BLESSING. THAT DAY...
"IT WAS THE BEGINNING OF A MIRACLE!
"A MIRACLE BECAUSE I AM BARREN -- UNABLE TO CONCEIVE A CHILD."

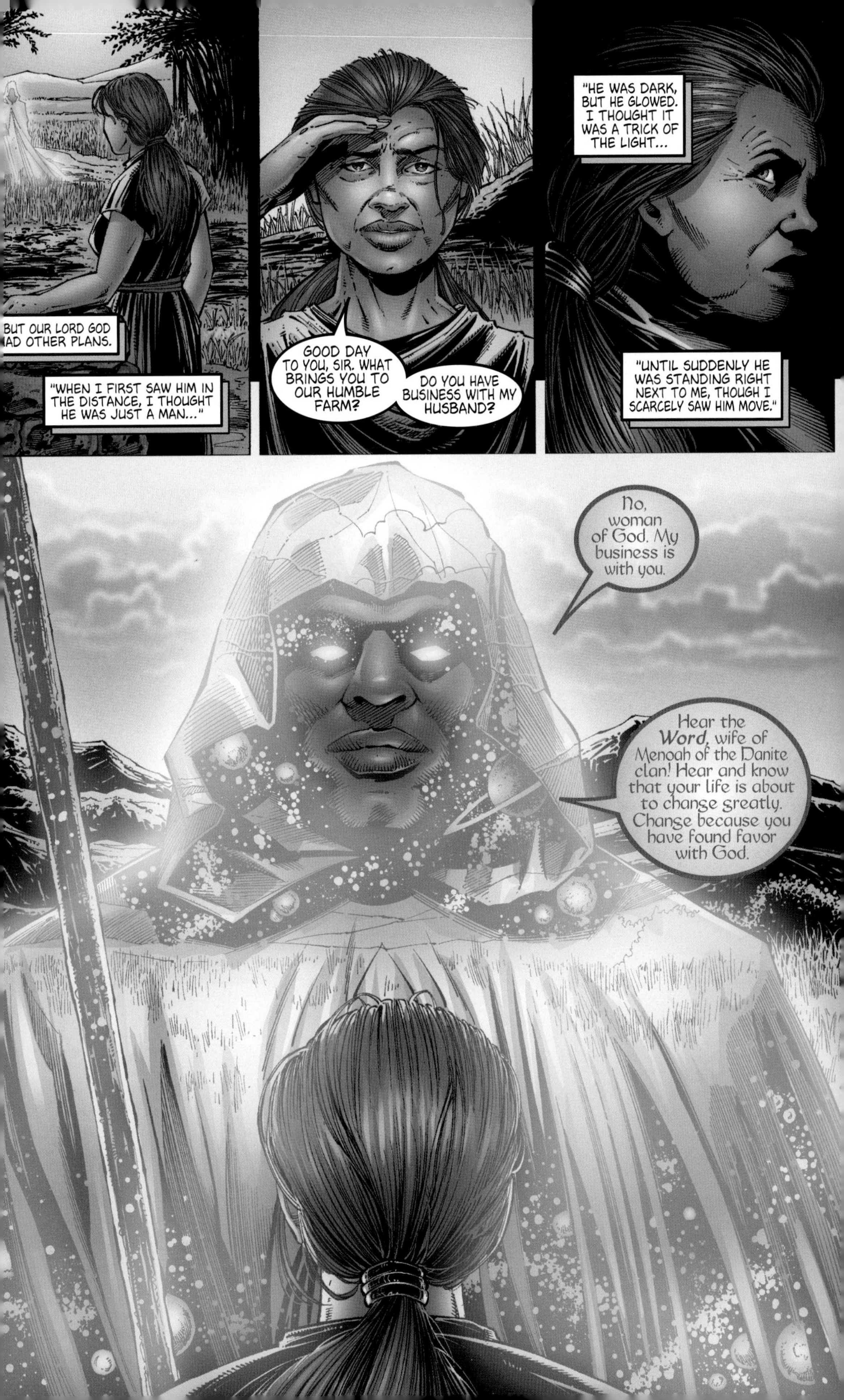

BUT OUR LORD GOD AD OTHER PLANS.
"WHEN I FIRST SAW HIM IN THE DISTANCE, I THOUGHT HE WAS JUST A MAN..."
GOOD DAY TO YOU, SIR. WHAT BRINGS YOU TO OUR HUMBLE FARM?
DO YOU HAVE BUSINESS WITH MY HUSBAND?
"HE WAS DARK, BUT HE GLOWED. I THOUGHT IT WAS A TRICK OF THE LIGHT...
"UNTIL SUDDENLY HE WAS STANDING RIGHT NEXT TO ME, THOUGH I SCARCELY SAW HIM MOVE."
No, woman of God. My business is with you.
Hear the **Word,** wife of Menoah of the Danite clan! Hear and know that your life is about to change greatly. Change because you have found favor with God.

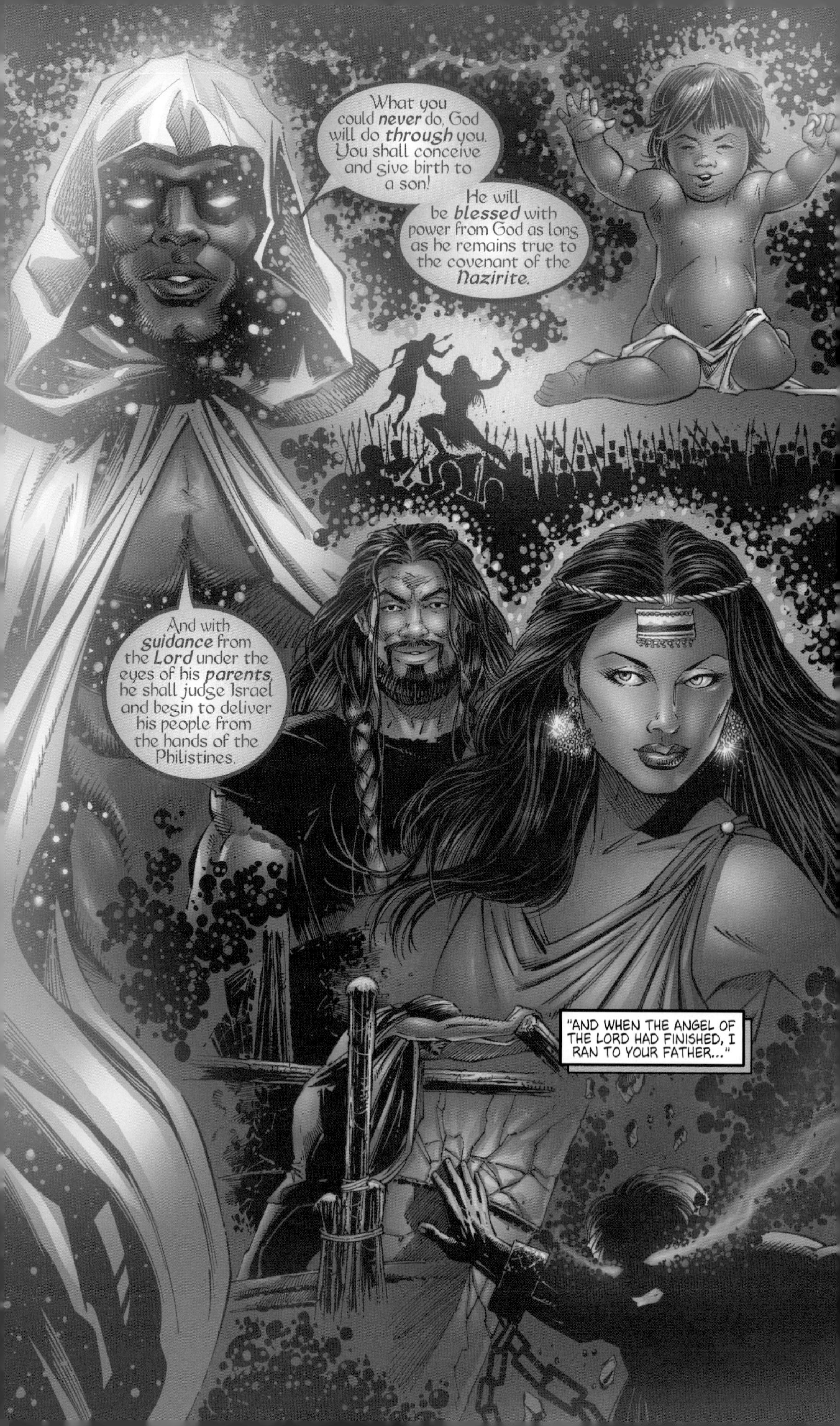
What you could never do, God will do through you. You shall conceive and give birth to a son!
He will be blessed with power from God as long as he remains true to the covenant of the Nazirite.
And with guidance from the Lord under the eyes of his parents, he shall judge Israel and begin to deliver his people from the hands of the Philistines.
"AND WHEN THE ANGEL OF THE LORD HAD FINISHED, I RAN TO YOUR FATHER..."

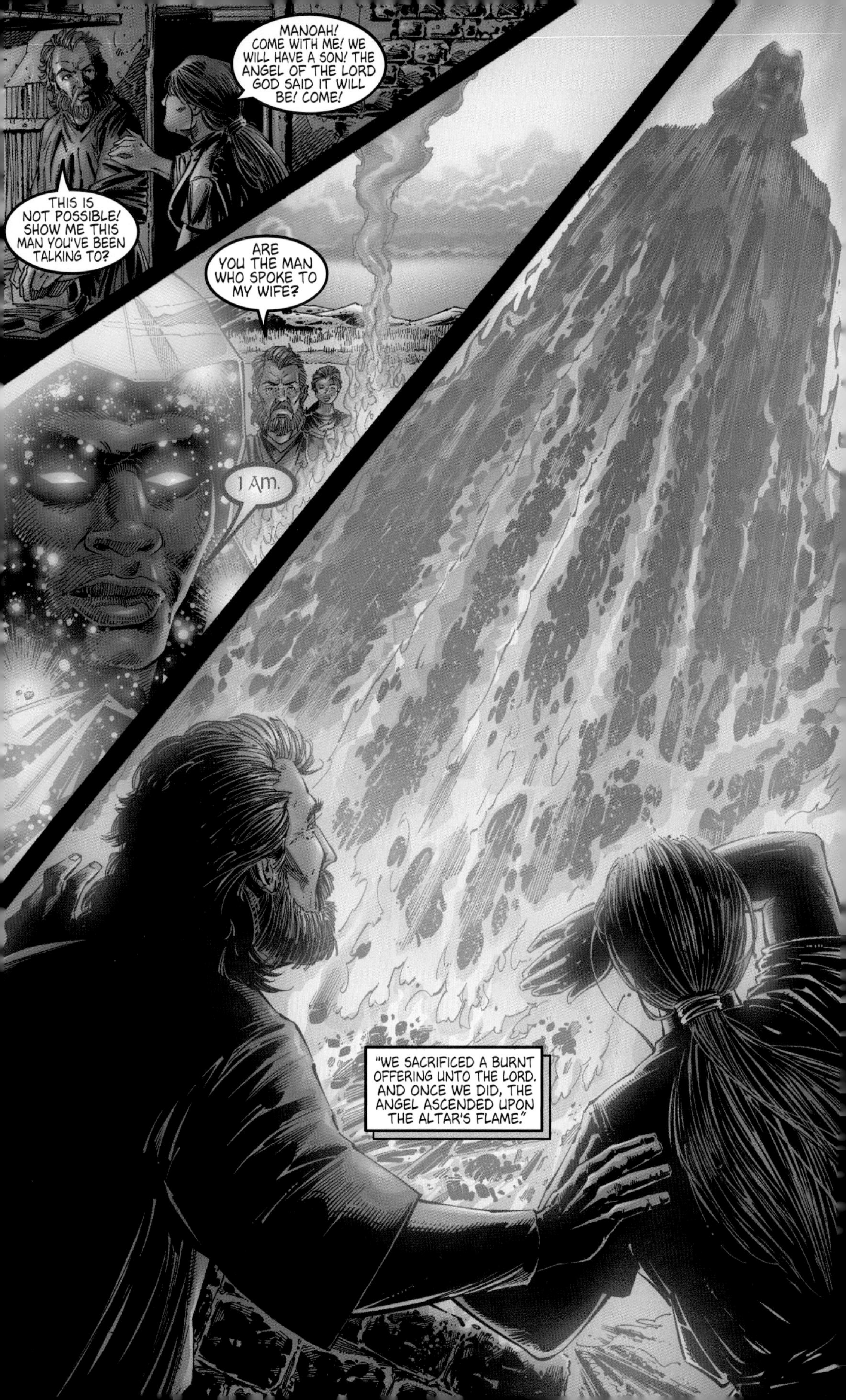
MANOAH! COME WITH ME! WE WILL HAVE A SON! THE ANGEL OF THE LORD GOD SAID IT WILL BE! COME!
THIS IS NOT POSSIBLE! SHOW ME THIS MAN YOU'VE BEEN TALKING TO?
ARE YOU THE MAN WHO SPOKE TO MY WIFE?
I AM.
"WE SACRIFICED A BURNT OFFERING UNTO THE LORD. AND ONCE WE DID, THE ANGEL ASCENDED UPON THE ALTAR'S FLAME."

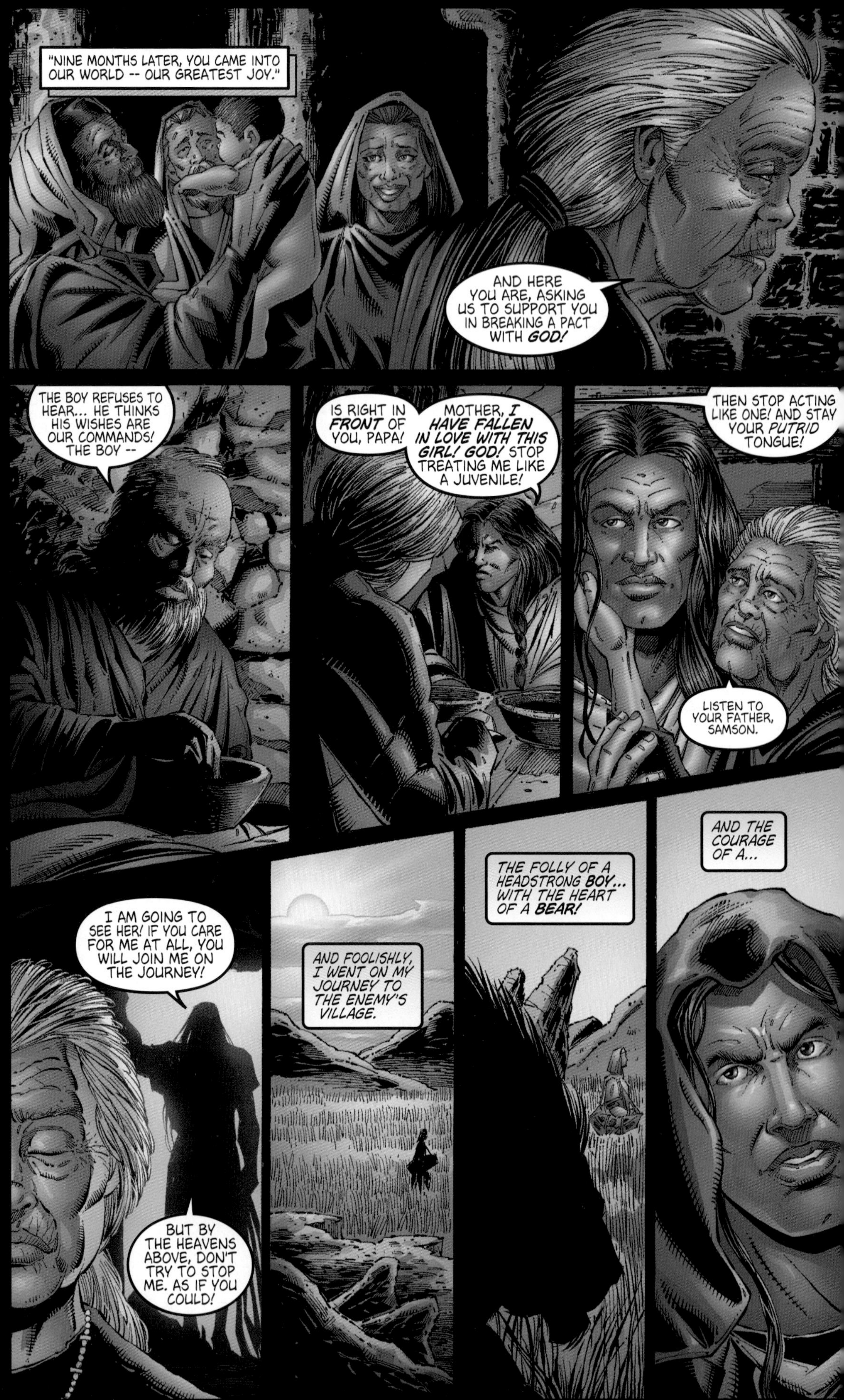

"NINE MONTHS LATER, YOU CAME INTO OUR WORLD -- OUR GREATEST JOY."
AND HERE YOU ARE, ASKING US TO SUPPORT YOU IN BREAKING A PACT WITH GOD!
THE BOY REFUSES TO HEAR... HE THINKS HIS WISHES ARE OUR COMMANDS! THE BOY --
IS RIGHT IN FRONT OF YOU, PAPA!
MOTHER, I HAVE FALLEN IN LOVE WITH THIS GIRL! GOD! STOP TREATING ME LIKE A JUVENILE!
THEN STOP ACTING LIKE ONE! AND STAY YOUR PUTRID TONGUE!
LISTEN TO YOUR FATHER, SAMSON.
I AM GOING TO SEE HER! IF YOU CARE FOR ME AT ALL, YOU WILL JOIN ME ON THE JOURNEY!
BUT BY THE HEAVENS ABOVE, DON'T TRY TO STOP ME. AS IF YOU COULD!
AND FOOLISHLY, I WENT ON MY JOURNEY TO THE ENEMY'S VILLAGE.
THE FOLLY OF A HEADSTRONG BOY... WITH THE HEART OF A BEAR!
AND THE COURAGE OF A...

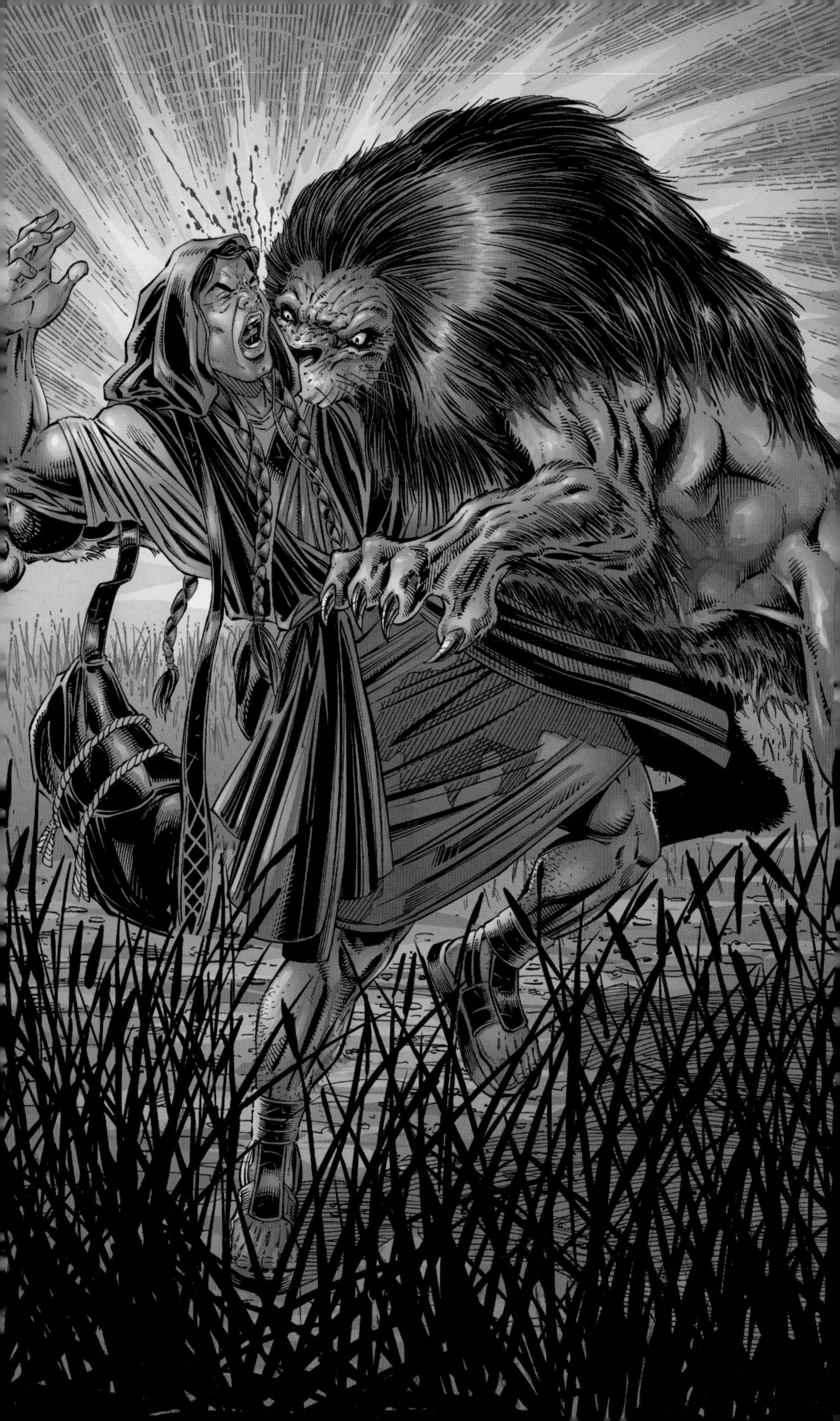

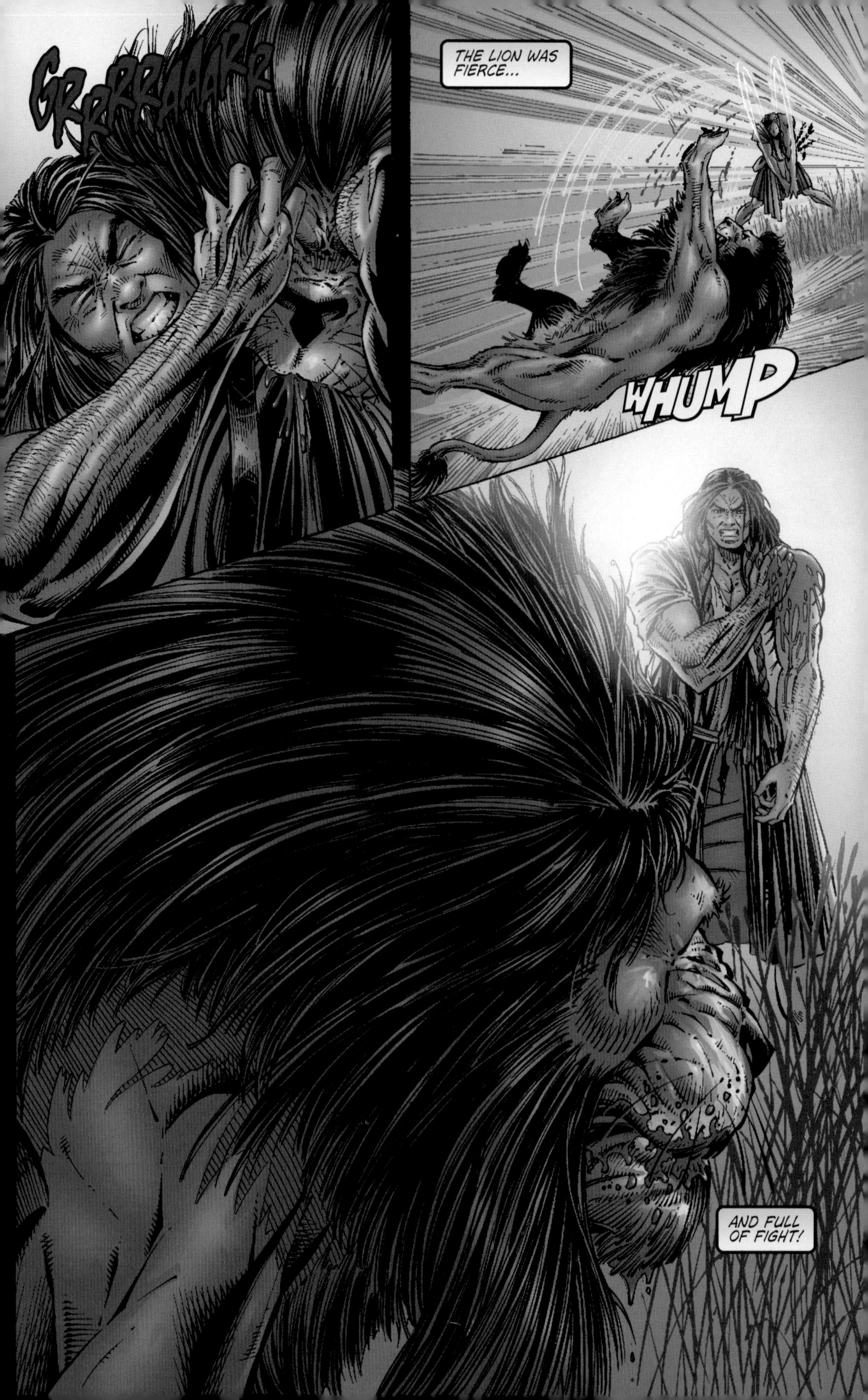
GRRRRAAARR
THE LION WAS FIERCE...
WHUMP
AND FULL OF FIGHT!

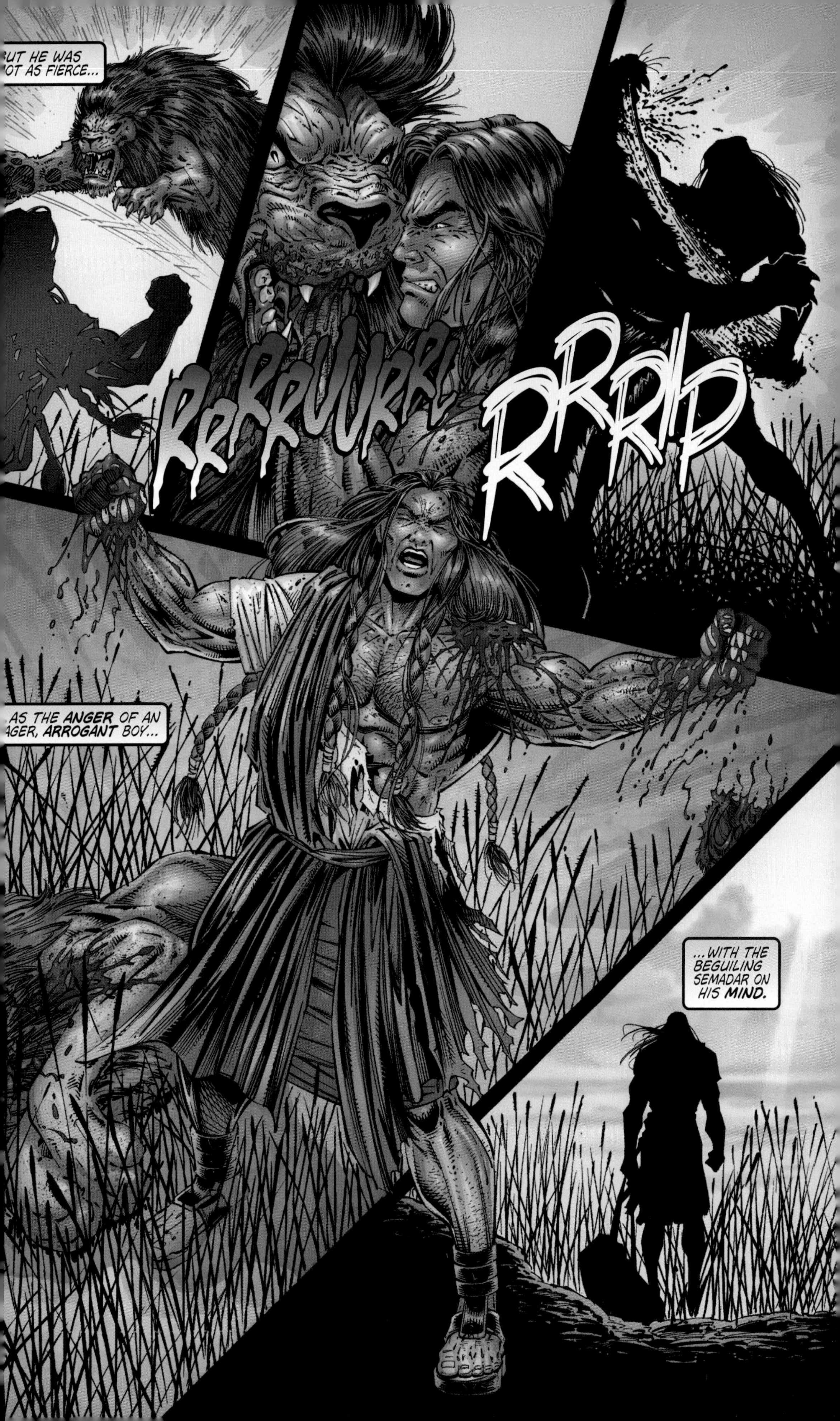

UT HE WAS
OT AS FIERCE...
RRRRUURRL
RRRIP
AS THE ANGER OF AN
AGER, ARROGANT BOY...
...WITH THE
BEGUILING
SEMADAR ON
HIS MIND.

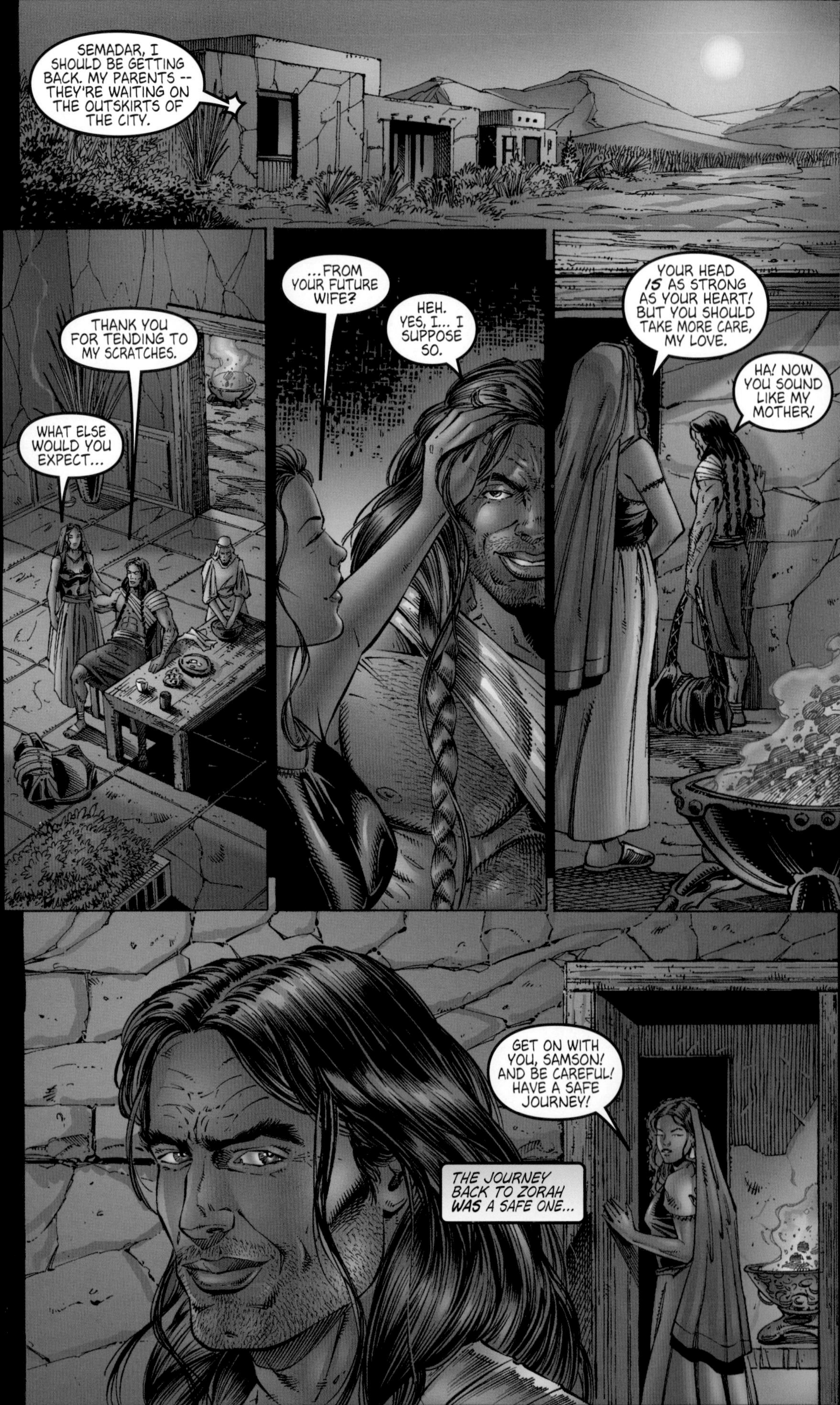
SEMADAR, I SHOULD BE GETTING BACK. MY PARENTS -- THEY'RE WAITING ON THE OUTSKIRTS OF THE CITY.
THANK YOU FOR TENDING TO MY SCRATCHES.
WHAT ELSE WOULD YOU EXPECT...
...FROM YOUR FUTURE WIFE?
HEH. YES, I... I SUPPOSE SO.
YOUR HEAD *IS* AS STRONG AS YOUR HEART! BUT YOU SHOULD TAKE MORE CARE, MY LOVE.
HA! NOW YOU SOUND LIKE MY MOTHER!
GET ON WITH YOU, SAMSON! AND BE CAREFUL! HAVE A SAFE JOURNEY!
THE JOURNEY BACK TO ZORAH ***WAS*** *A SAFE ONE...*

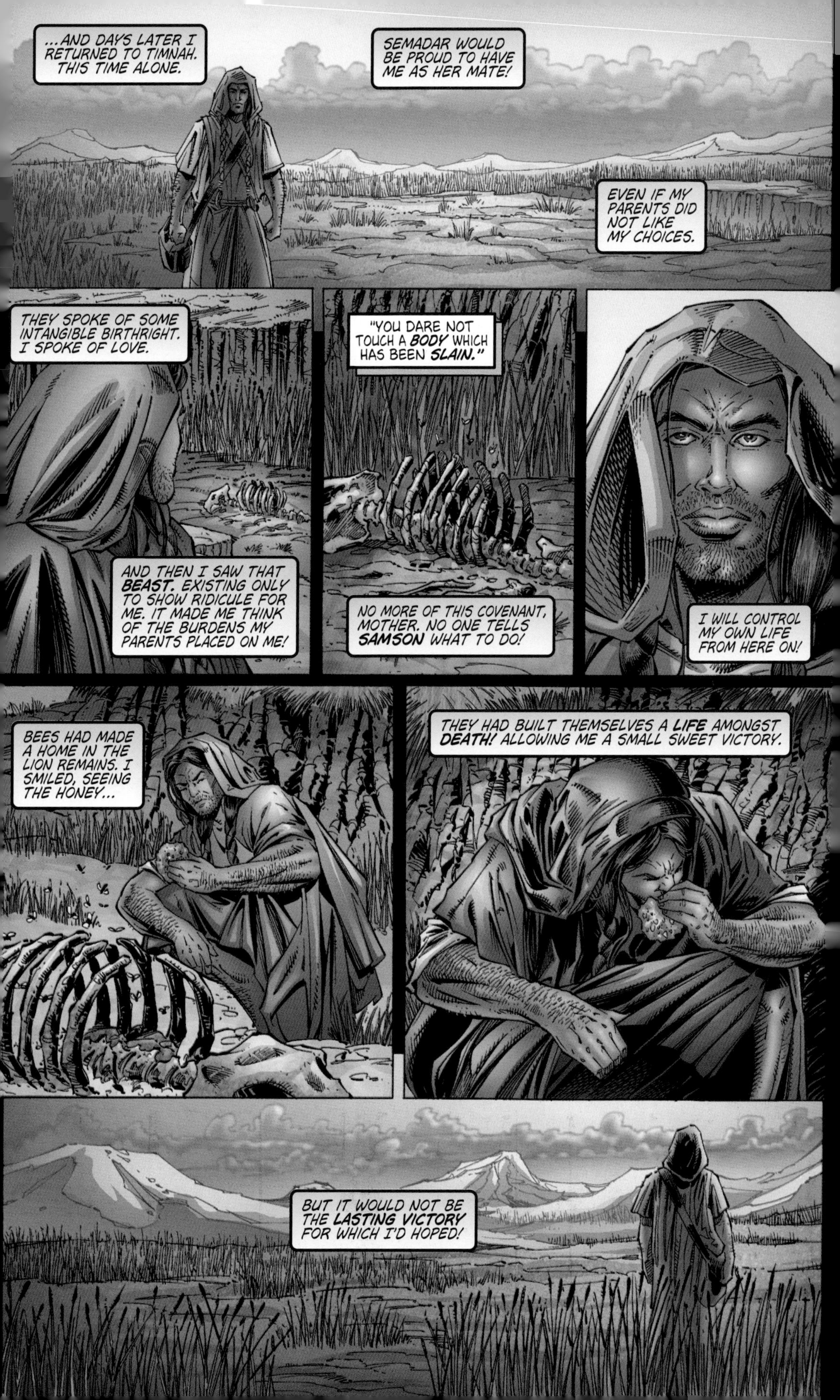
...AND DAYS LATER I RETURNED TO TIMNAH. THIS TIME ALONE.
SEMADAR WOULD BE PROUD TO HAVE ME AS HER MATE!
EVEN IF MY PARENTS DID NOT LIKE MY CHOICES.
THEY SPOKE OF SOME INTANGIBLE BIRTHRIGHT. I SPOKE OF LOVE.
AND THEN I SAW THAT **BEAST.** EXISTING ONLY TO SHOW RIDICULE FOR ME. IT MADE ME THINK OF THE BURDENS MY PARENTS PLACED ON ME!
"YOU DARE NOT TOUCH A **BODY** WHICH HAS BEEN **SLAIN.**"
NO MORE OF THIS COVENANT, MOTHER. NO ONE TELLS **SAMSON** WHAT TO DO!
I WILL CONTROL MY OWN LIFE FROM HERE ON!
BEES HAD MADE A HOME IN THE LION REMAINS. I SMILED, SEEING THE HONEY...
THEY HAD BUILT THEMSELVES A **LIFE** AMONGST **DEATH!** ALLOWING ME A SMALL SWEET VICTORY.
BUT IT WOULD NOT BE THE **LASTING VICTORY** FOR WHICH I'D HOPED!

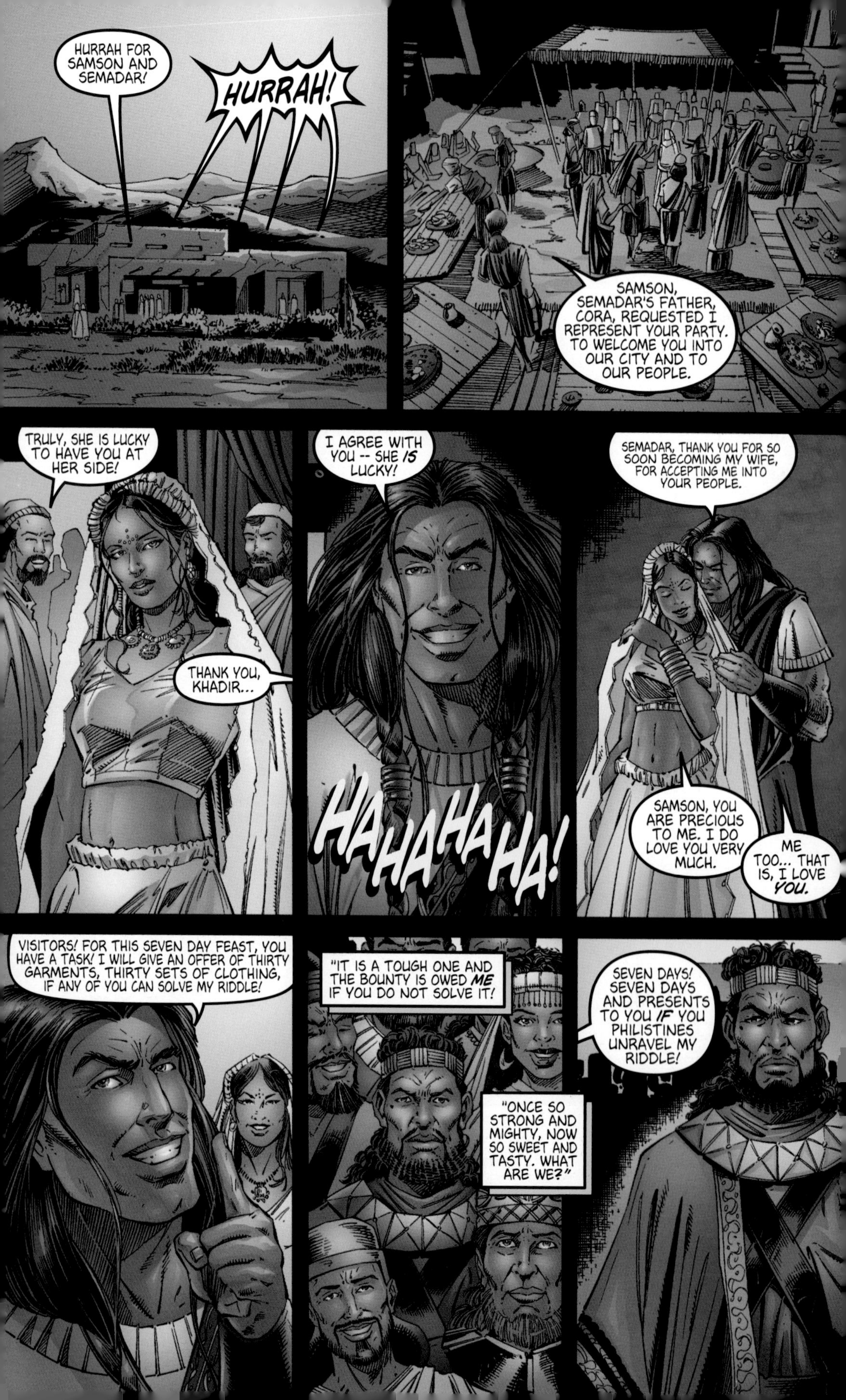
HURRAH FOR SAMSON AND SEMADAR!
HURRAH!
SAMSON, SEMADAR'S FATHER, CORA, REQUESTED I REPRESENT YOUR PARTY. TO WELCOME YOU INTO OUR CITY AND TO OUR PEOPLE.
TRULY, SHE IS LUCKY TO HAVE YOU AT HER SIDE!
THANK YOU, KHADIR...
I AGREE WITH YOU -- SHE *IS* LUCKY!
HAHAHAHAHA!
SEMADAR, THANK YOU FOR SO SOON BECOMING MY WIFE, FOR ACCEPTING ME INTO YOUR PEOPLE.
SAMSON, YOU ARE PRECIOUS TO ME. I DO LOVE YOU VERY MUCH.
ME TOO... THAT IS, I LOVE *YOU.*
VISITORS! FOR THIS SEVEN DAY FEAST, YOU HAVE A TASK! I WILL GIVE AN OFFER OF THIRTY GARMENTS, THIRTY SETS OF CLOTHING, IF ANY OF YOU CAN SOLVE MY RIDDLE!
"IT IS A TOUGH ONE AND THE BOUNTY IS OWED *ME* IF YOU DO NOT SOLVE IT!
"ONCE SO STRONG AND MIGHTY, NOW SO SWEET AND TASTY. WHAT ARE WE?"
SEVEN DAYS! SEVEN DAYS AND PRESENTS TO YOU *IF* YOU PHILISTINES UNRAVEL MY RIDDLE!

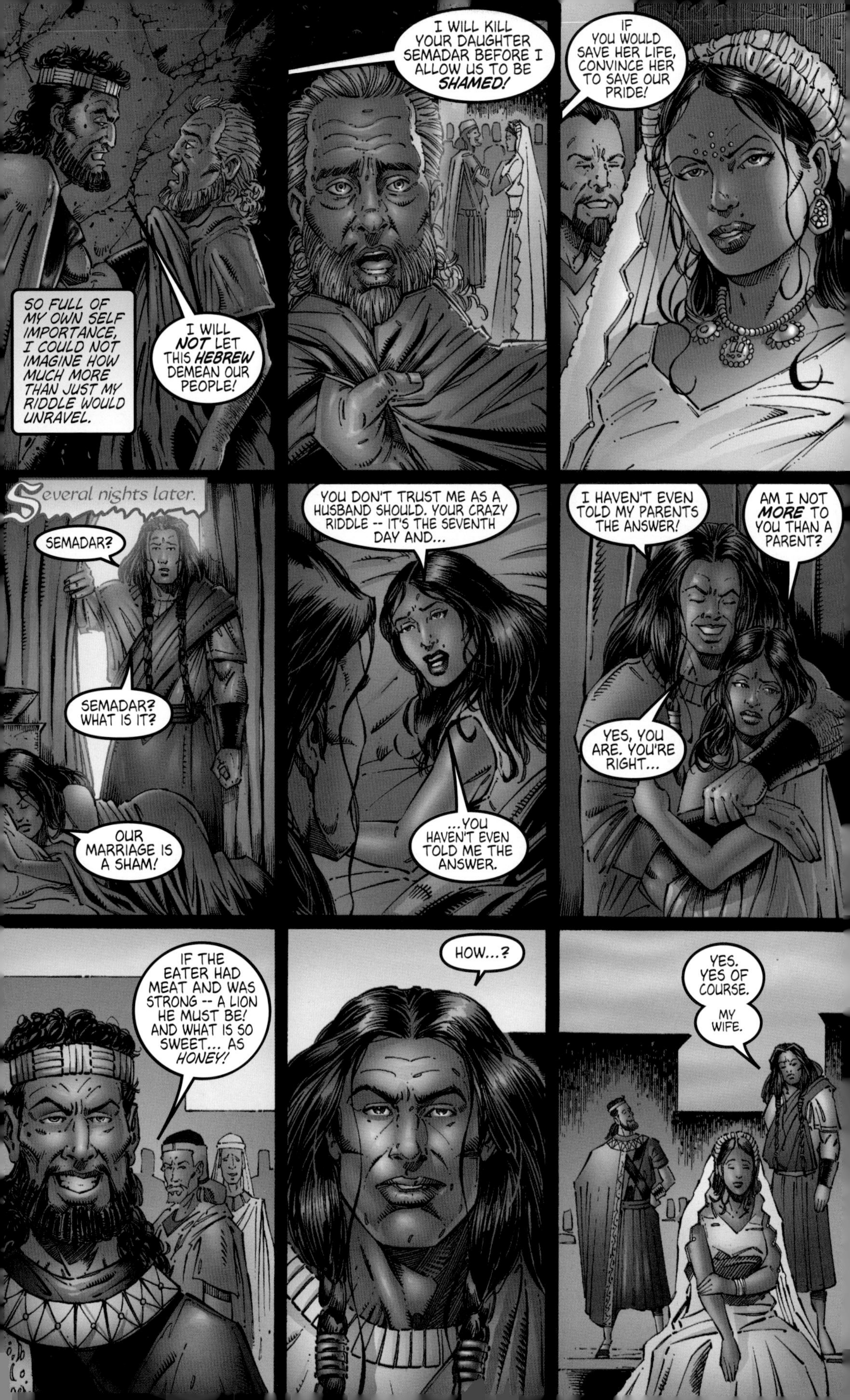
SO FULL OF MY OWN SELF IMPORTANCE, I COULD NOT IMAGINE HOW MUCH MORE THAN JUST MY RIDDLE WOULD UNRAVEL.
I WILL NOT LET THIS HEBREW DEMEAN OUR PEOPLE!
I WILL KILL YOUR DAUGHTER SEMADAR BEFORE I ALLOW US TO BE SHAMED!
IF YOU WOULD SAVE HER LIFE, CONVINCE HER TO SAVE OUR PRIDE!
Several nights later.
SEMADAR?
SEMADAR? WHAT IS IT?
OUR MARRIAGE IS A SHAM!
YOU DON'T TRUST ME AS A HUSBAND SHOULD. YOUR CRAZY RIDDLE -- IT'S THE SEVENTH DAY AND...
...YOU HAVEN'T EVEN TOLD ME THE ANSWER.
I HAVEN'T EVEN TOLD MY PARENTS THE ANSWER!
AM I NOT MORE TO YOU THAN A PARENT?
YES, YOU ARE. YOU'RE RIGHT...
IF THE EATER HAD MEAT AND WAS STRONG -- A LION HE MUST BE! AND WHAT IS SO SWEET... AS HONEY!
HOW...?
YES. YES OF COURSE.
MY WIFE.

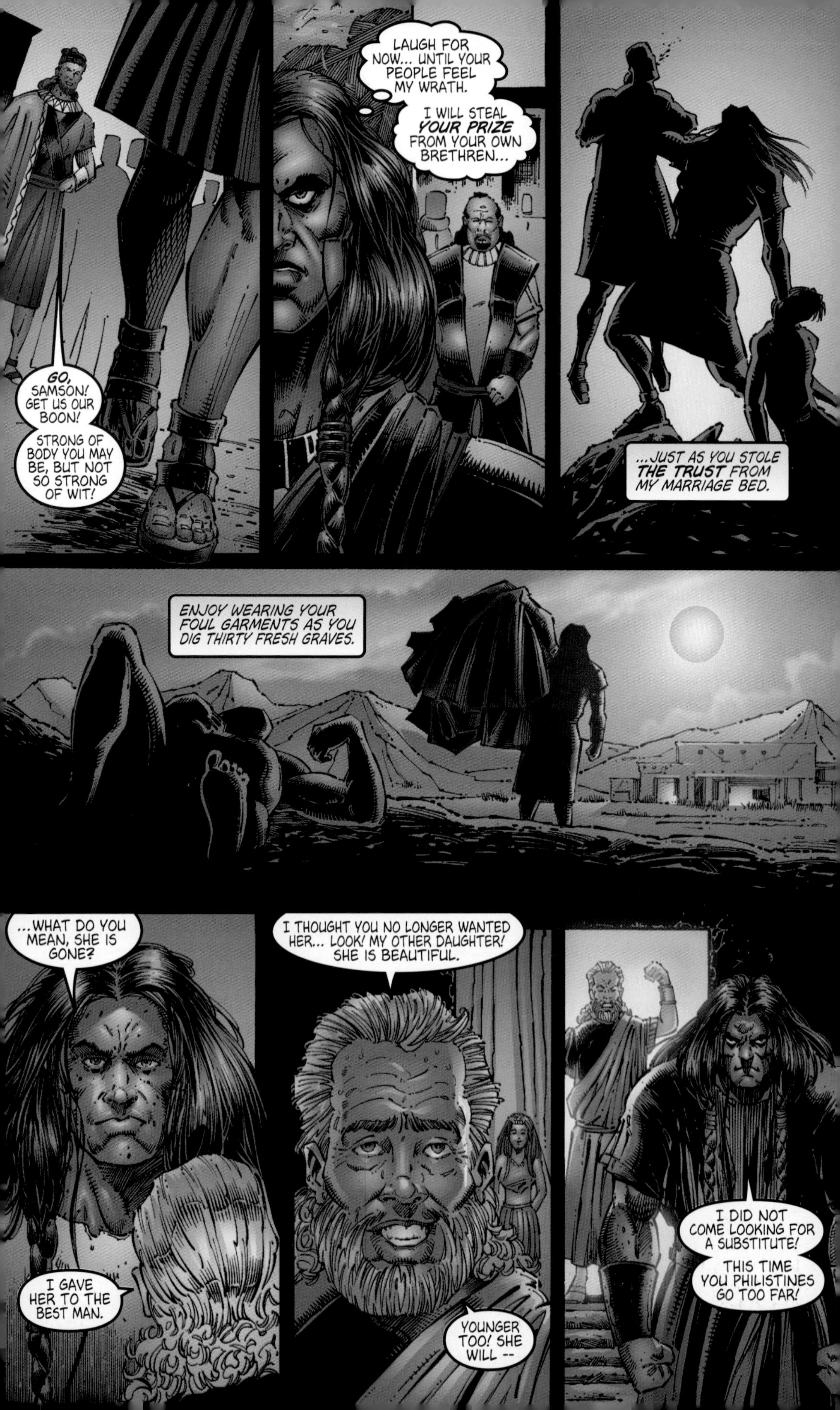

GO, SAMSON! GET US OUR BOON!
STRONG OF BODY YOU MAY BE, BUT NOT SO STRONG OF WIT!
LAUGH FOR NOW... UNTIL YOUR PEOPLE FEEL MY WRATH.
I WILL STEAL YOUR PRIZE FROM YOUR OWN BRETHREN...
...JUST AS YOU STOLE THE TRUST FROM MY MARRIAGE BED.
ENJOY WEARING YOUR FOUL GARMENTS AS YOU DIG THIRTY FRESH GRAVES.
...WHAT DO YOU MEAN, SHE IS GONE?
I GAVE HER TO THE BEST MAN.
I THOUGHT YOU NO LONGER WANTED HER... LOOK! MY OTHER DAUGHTER! SHE IS BEAUTIFUL.
YOUNGER TOO! SHE WILL --
I DID NOT COME LOOKING FOR A SUBSTITUTE!
THIS TIME YOU PHILISTINES GO TOO FAR!

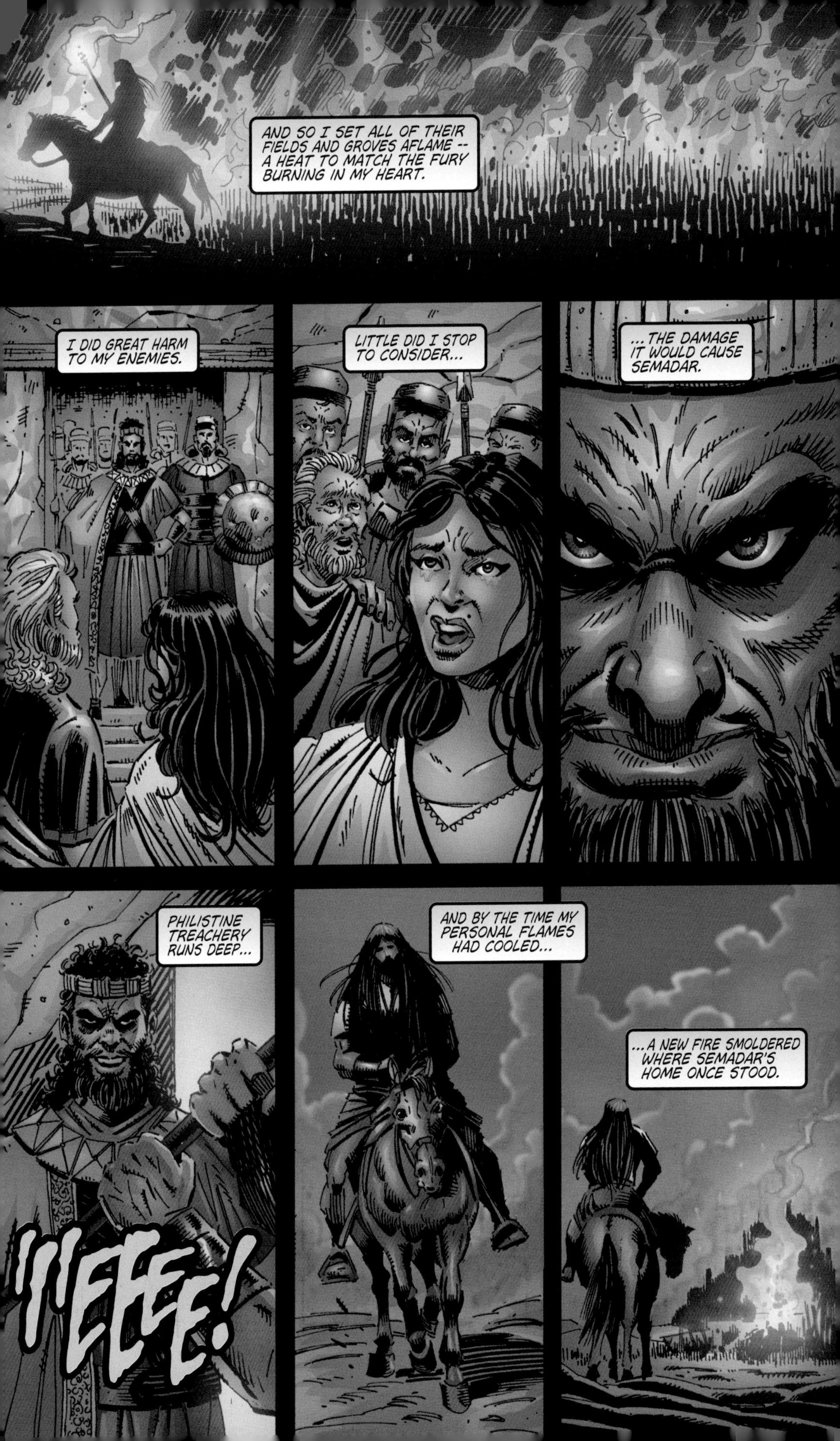
AND SO I SET ALL OF THEIR FIELDS AND GROVES AFLAME -- A HEAT TO MATCH THE FURY BURNING IN MY HEART.
I DID GREAT HARM TO MY ENEMIES.
LITTLE DID I STOP TO CONSIDER...
...THE DAMAGE IT WOULD CAUSE SEMADAR.
PHILISTINE TREACHERY RUNS DEEP...
IIEEEE!
AND BY THE TIME MY PERSONAL FLAMES HAD COOLED...
...A NEW FIRE SMOLDERED WHERE SEMADAR'S HOME ONCE STOOD.

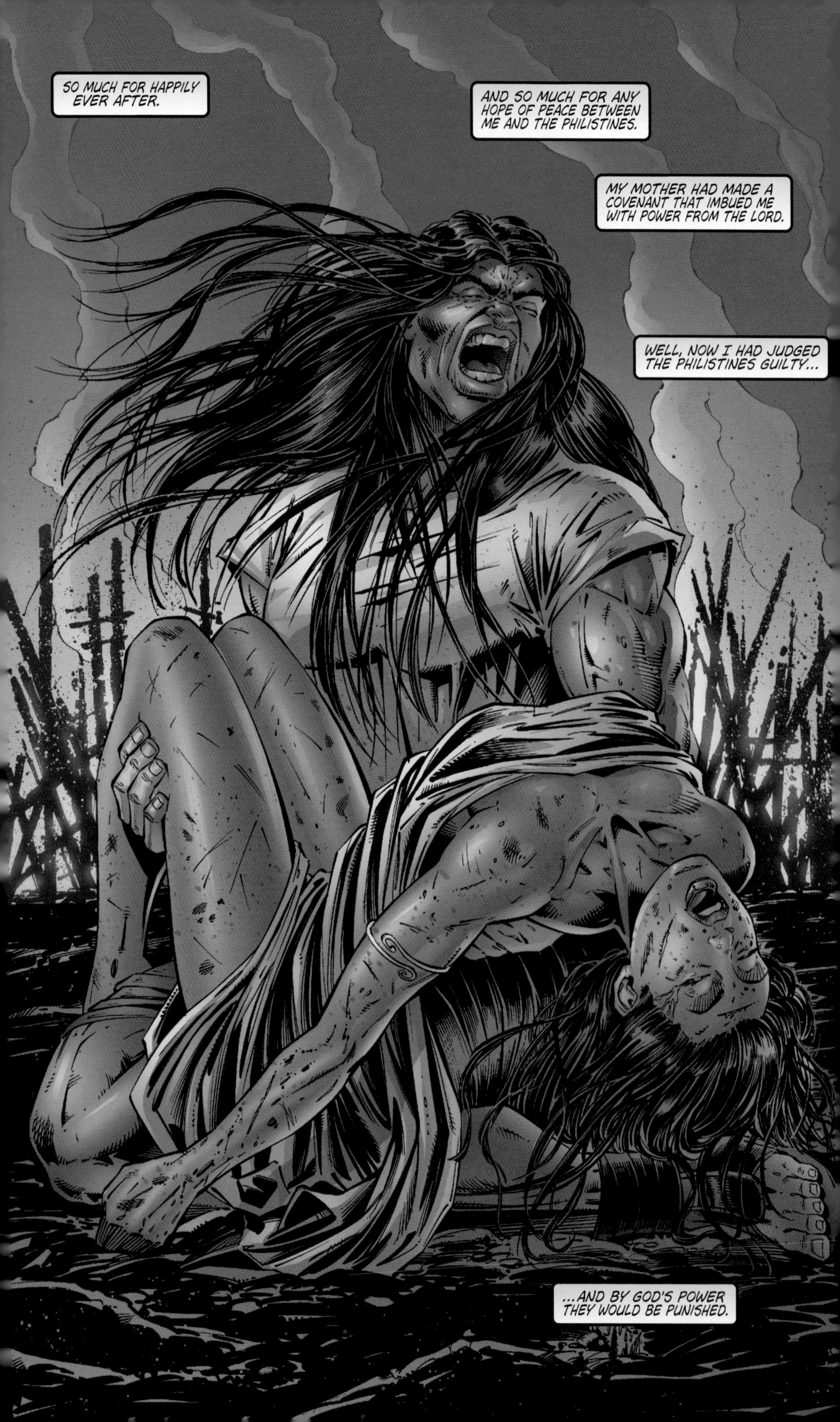
SO MUCH FOR HAPPILY EVER AFTER.
AND SO MUCH FOR ANY HOPE OF PEACE BETWEEN ME AND THE PHILISTINES.
MY MOTHER HAD MADE A COVENANT THAT IMBUED ME WITH POWER FROM THE LORD.
WELL, NOW I HAD JUDGED THE PHILISTINES GUILTY...
...AND BY GOD'S POWER THEY WOULD BE PUNISHED.

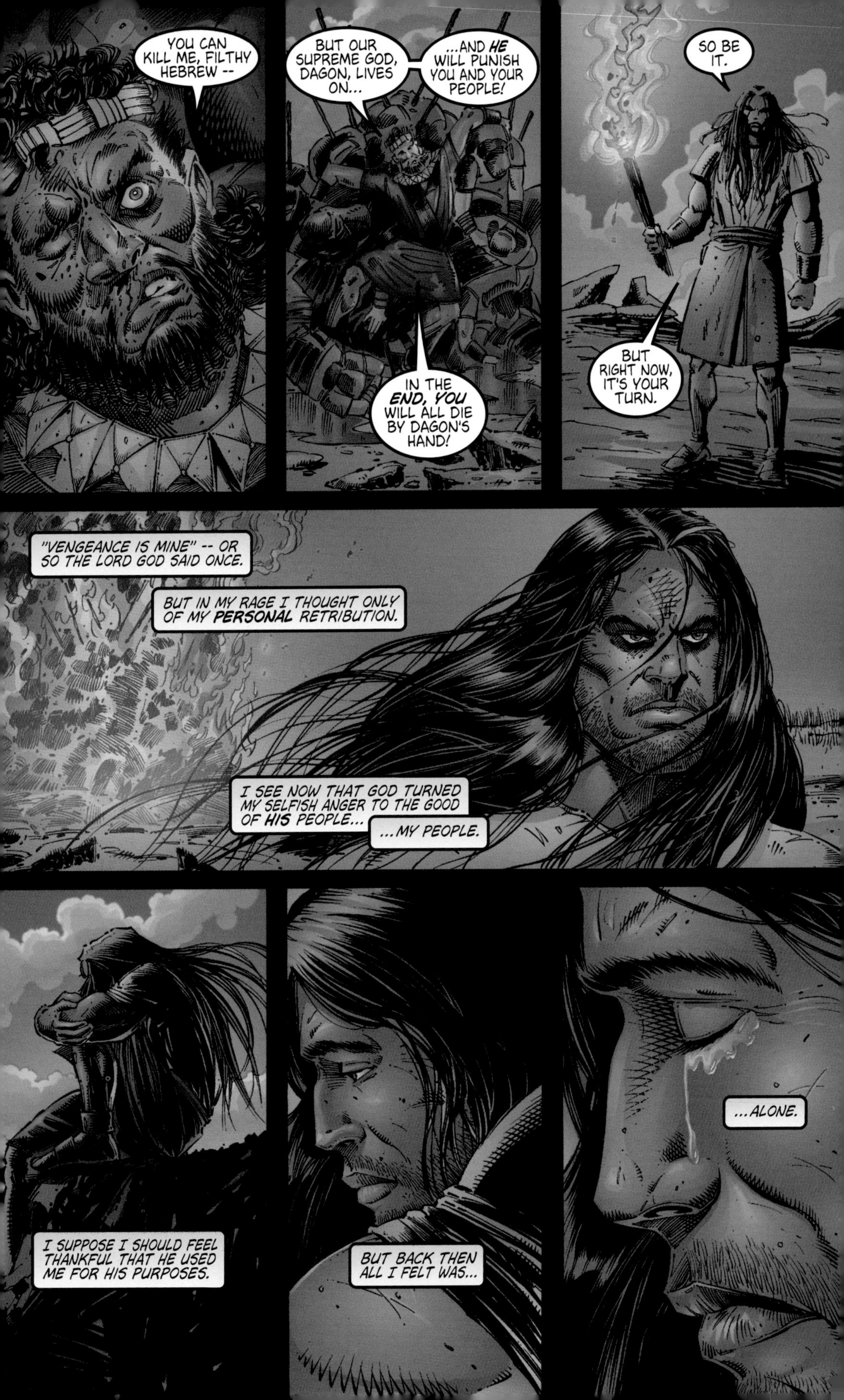
YOU CAN KILL ME, FILTHY HEBREW --
BUT OUR SUPREME GOD, DAGON, LIVES ON...
...AND HE WILL PUNISH YOU AND YOUR PEOPLE!
IN THE END, YOU WILL ALL DIE BY DAGON'S HAND!
SO BE IT.
BUT RIGHT NOW, IT'S YOUR TURN.
"VENGEANCE IS MINE" -- OR SO THE LORD GOD SAID ONCE.
BUT IN MY RAGE I THOUGHT ONLY OF MY PERSONAL RETRIBUTION.
I SEE NOW THAT GOD TURNED MY SELFISH ANGER TO THE GOOD OF HIS PEOPLE...
...MY PEOPLE.
I SUPPOSE I SHOULD FEEL THANKFUL THAT HE USED ME FOR HIS PURPOSES.
BUT BACK THEN ALL I FELT WAS...
...ALONE.

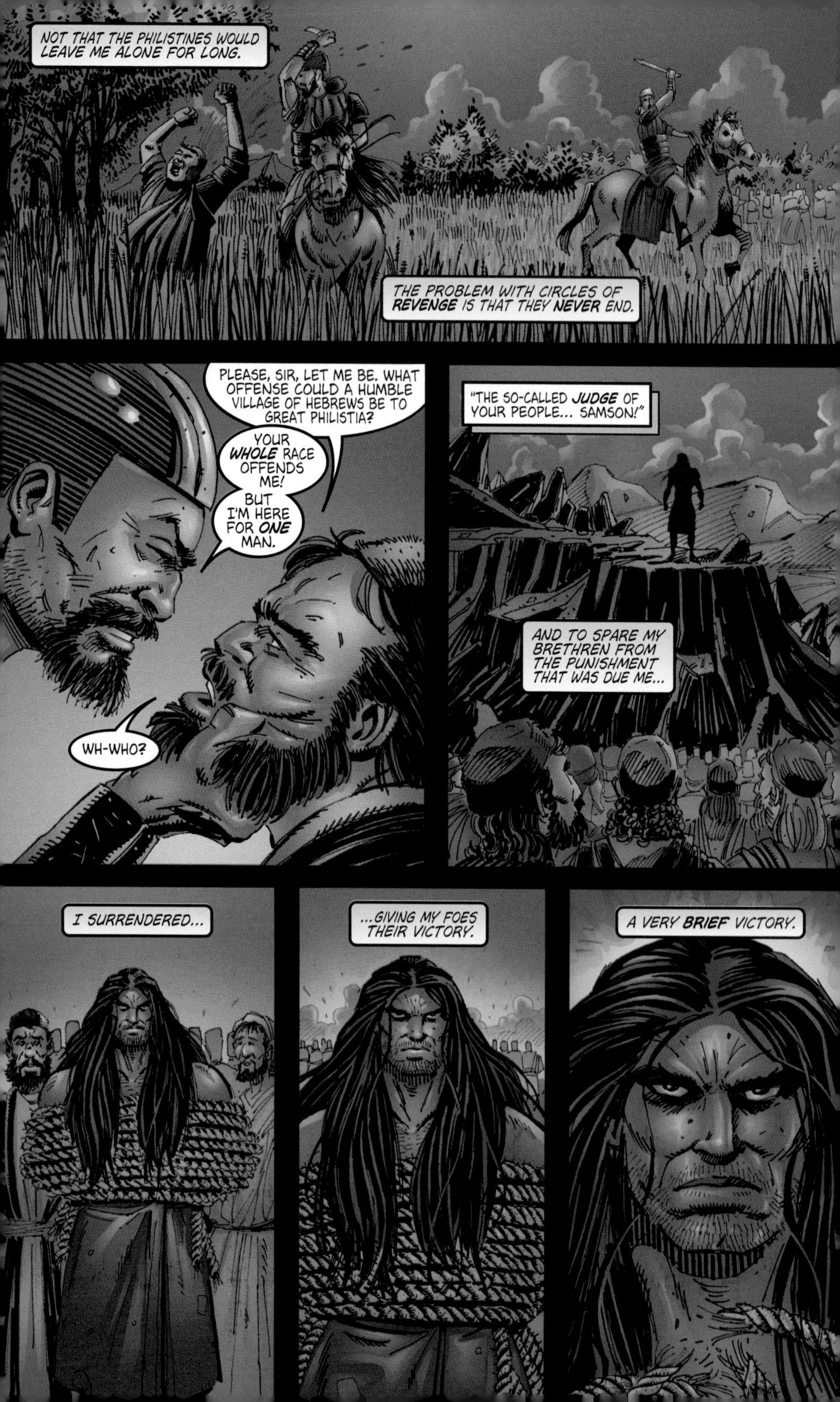
NOT THAT THE PHILISTINES WOULD LEAVE ME ALONE FOR LONG.
THE PROBLEM WITH CIRCLES OF REVENGE IS THAT THEY NEVER END.
PLEASE, SIR, LET ME BE. WHAT OFFENSE COULD A HUMBLE VILLAGE OF HEBREWS BE TO GREAT PHILISTIA?
YOUR WHOLE RACE OFFENDS ME!
BUT I'M HERE FOR ONE MAN.
WH-WHO?
"THE SO-CALLED JUDGE OF YOUR PEOPLE... SAMSON!"
AND TO SPARE MY BRETHREN FROM THE PUNISHMENT THAT WAS DUE ME...
I SURRENDERED...
...GIVING MY FOES THEIR VICTORY.
A VERY BRIEF VICTORY.

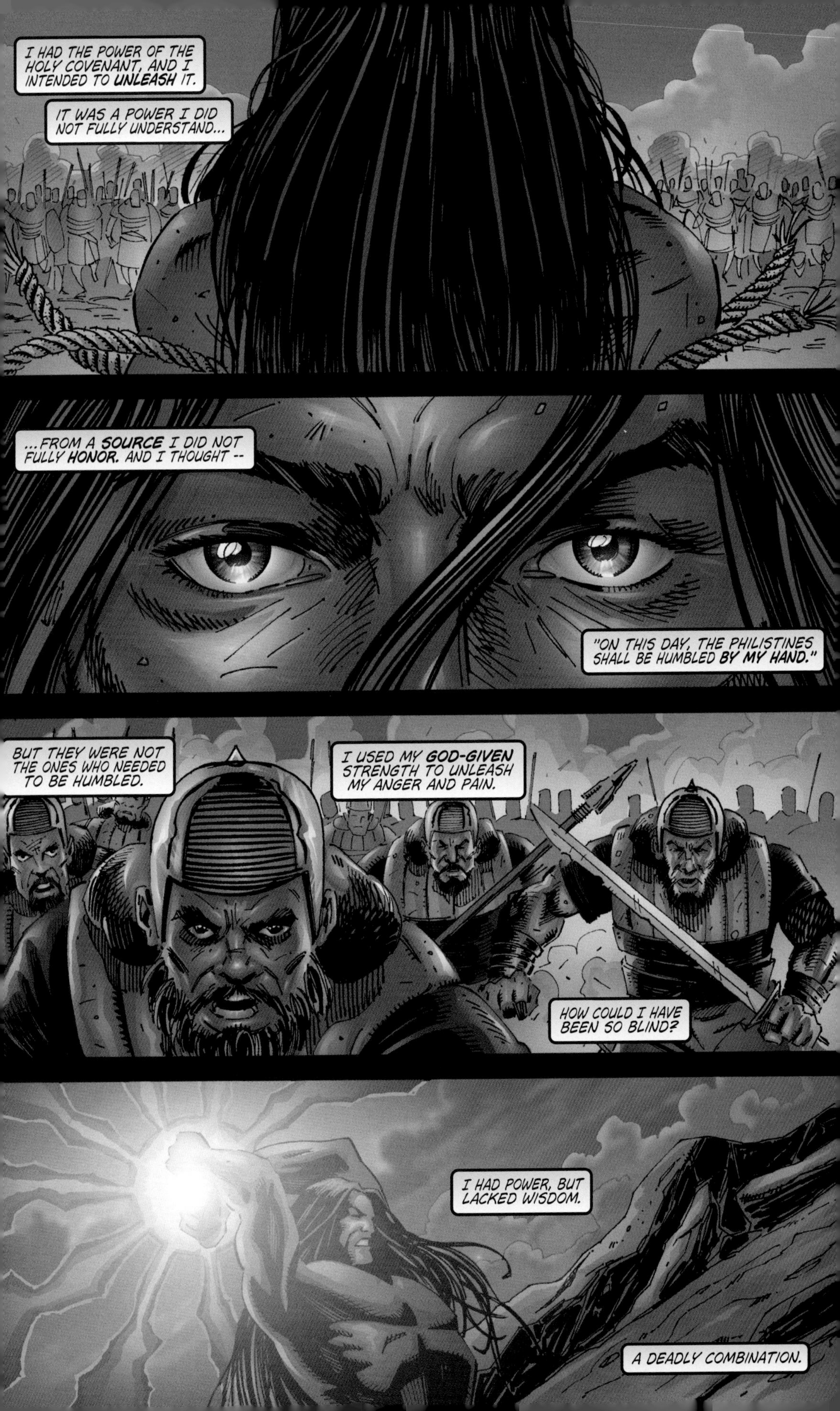
I HAD THE POWER OF THE HOLY COVENANT, AND I INTENDED TO UNLEASH IT.
IT WAS A POWER I DID NOT FULLY UNDERSTAND...
...FROM A SOURCE I DID NOT FULLY HONOR. AND I THOUGHT --
"ON THIS DAY, THE PHILISTINES SHALL BE HUMBLED BY MY HAND."
BUT THEY WERE NOT THE ONES WHO NEEDED TO BE HUMBLED.
I USED MY GOD-GIVEN STRENGTH TO UNLEASH MY ANGER AND PAIN.
HOW COULD I HAVE BEEN SO BLIND?
I HAD POWER, BUT LACKED WISDOM.
A DEADLY COMBINATION.

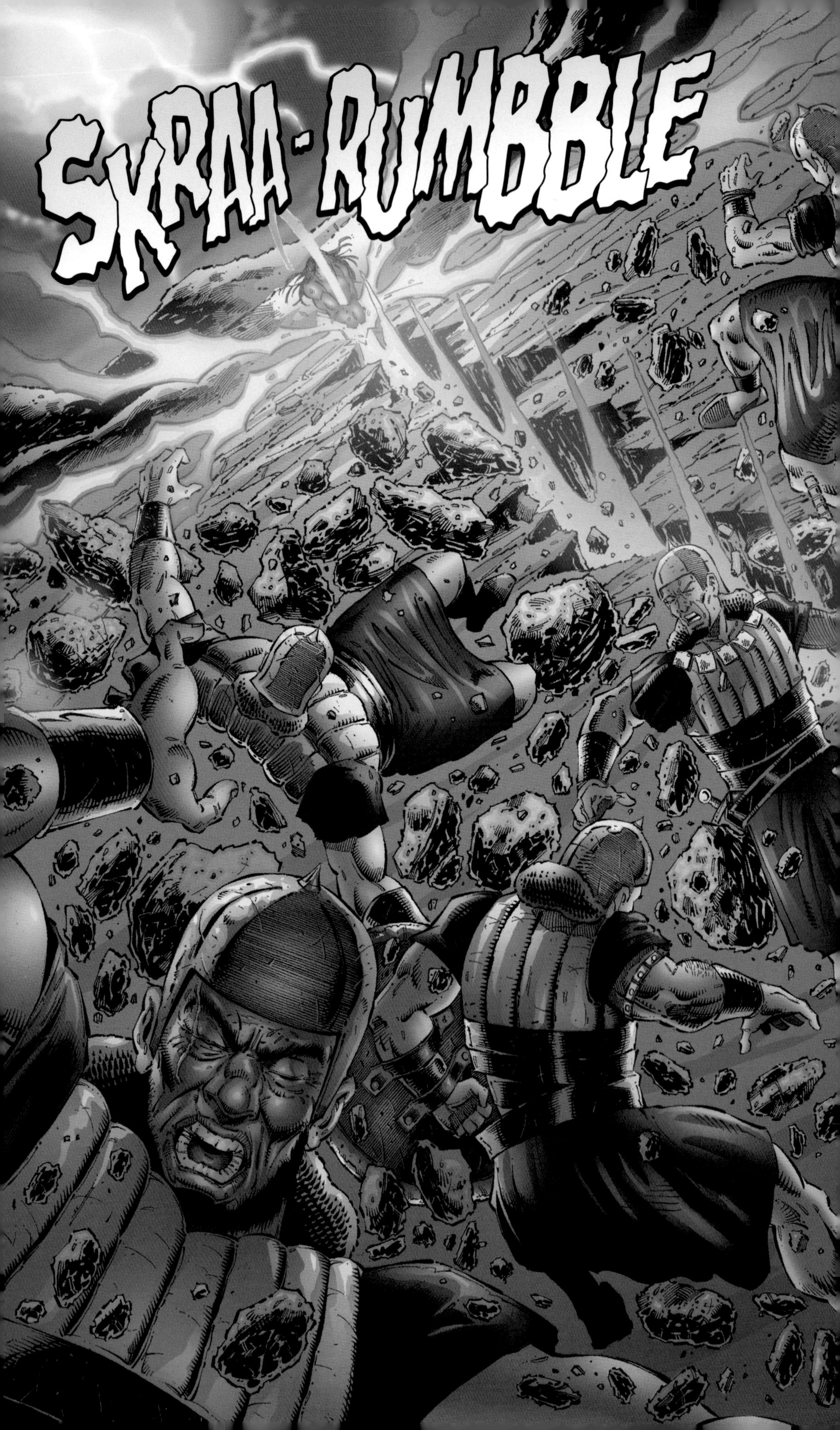
SKRAA-RUMBBLE

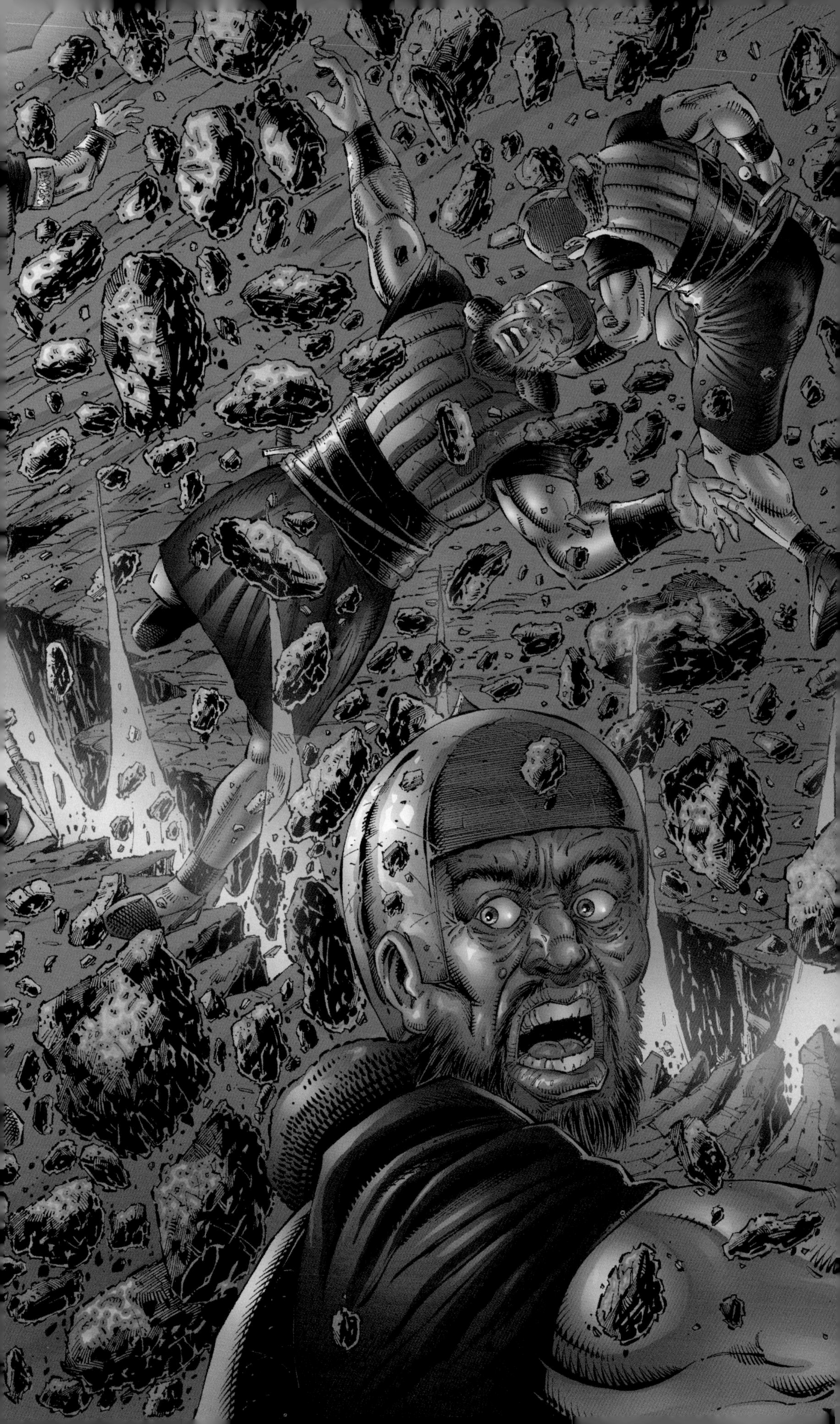

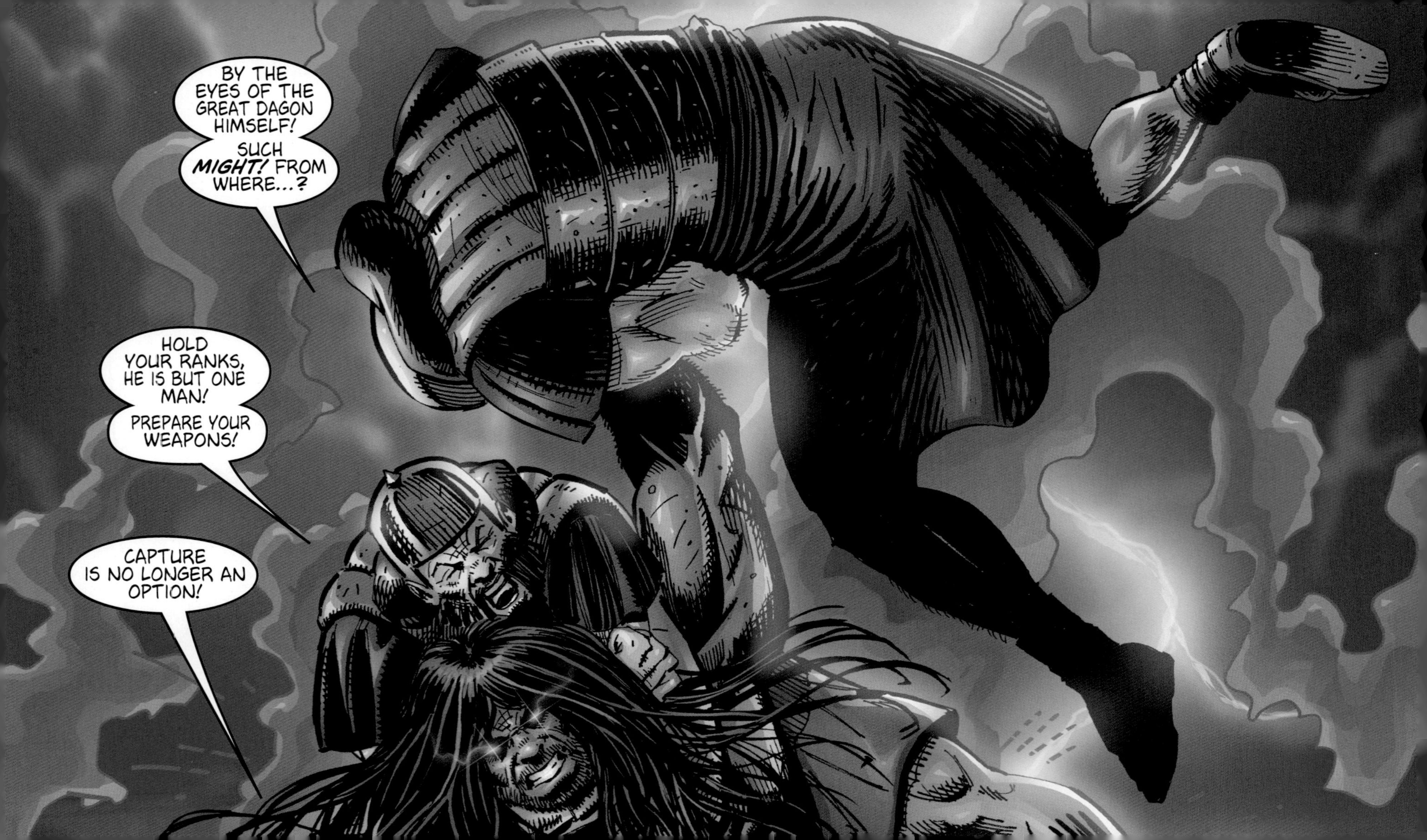
BY THE EYES OF THE GREAT DAGON HIMSELF!
SUCH **MIGHT!** FROM WHERE...?
HOLD YOUR RANKS, HE IS BUT ONE MAN!
PREPARE YOUR WEAPONS!
CAPTURE IS NO LONGER AN OPTION!

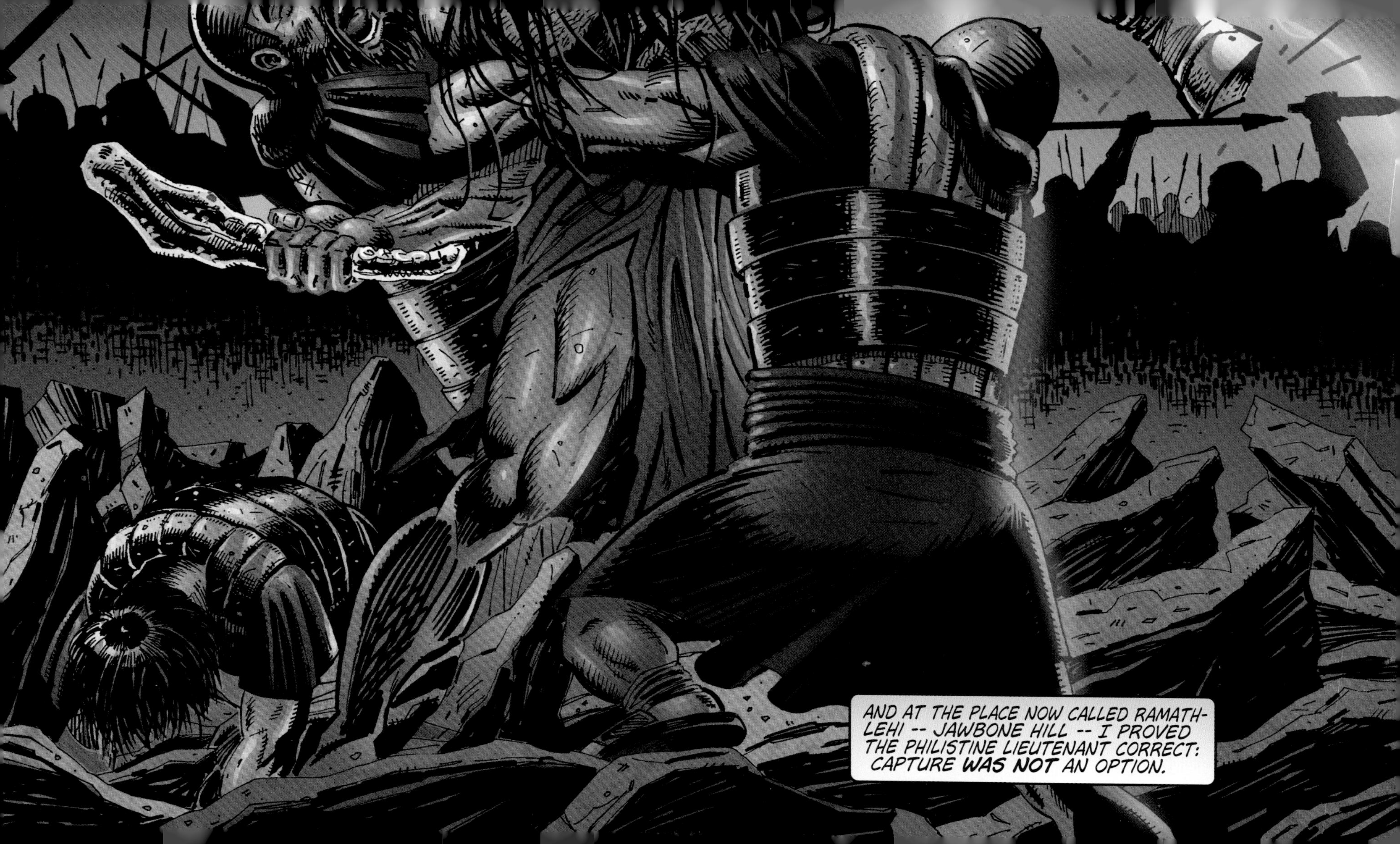
AND AT THE PLACE NOW CALLED RAMATH-LEHI -- JAWBONE HILL -- I PROVED THE PHILISTINE LIEUTENANT CORRECT: CAPTURE **WAS NOT** AN OPTION.

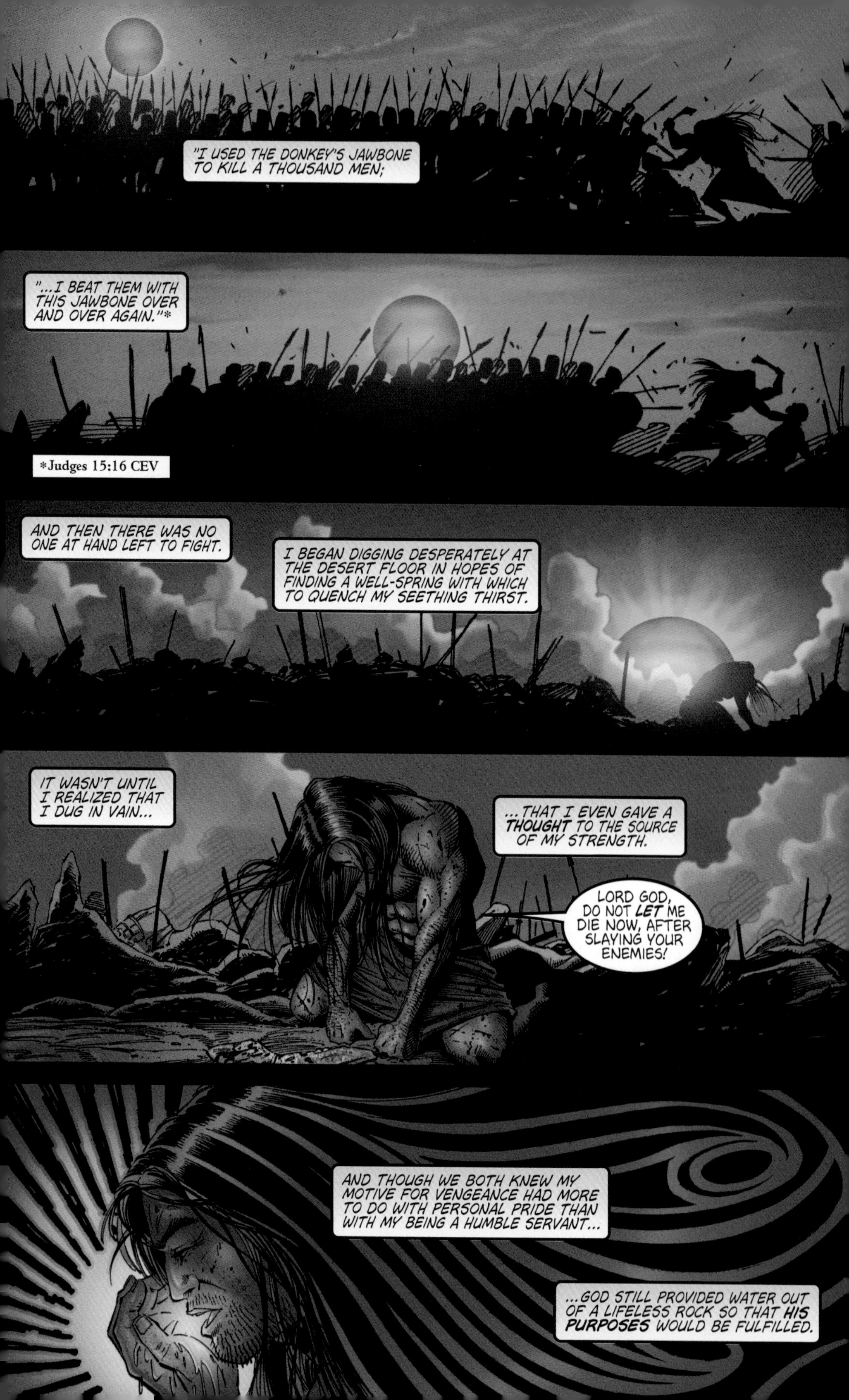
"I USED THE DONKEY'S JAWBONE TO KILL A THOUSAND MEN;
"...I BEAT THEM WITH THIS JAWBONE OVER AND OVER AGAIN."*
*Judges 15:16 CEV
AND THEN THERE WAS NO ONE AT HAND LEFT TO FIGHT.
I BEGAN DIGGING DESPERATELY AT THE DESERT FLOOR IN HOPES OF FINDING A WELL-SPRING WITH WHICH TO QUENCH MY SEETHING THIRST.
IT WASN'T UNTIL I REALIZED THAT I DUG IN VAIN...
...THAT I EVEN GAVE A THOUGHT TO THE SOURCE OF MY STRENGTH.
LORD GOD, DO NOT LET ME DIE NOW, AFTER SLAYING YOUR ENEMIES!
AND THOUGH WE BOTH KNEW MY MOTIVE FOR VENGEANCE HAD MORE TO DO WITH PERSONAL PRIDE THAN WITH MY BEING A HUMBLE SERVANT...
...GOD STILL PROVIDED WATER OUT OF A LIFELESS ROCK SO THAT HIS PURPOSES WOULD BE FULFILLED.

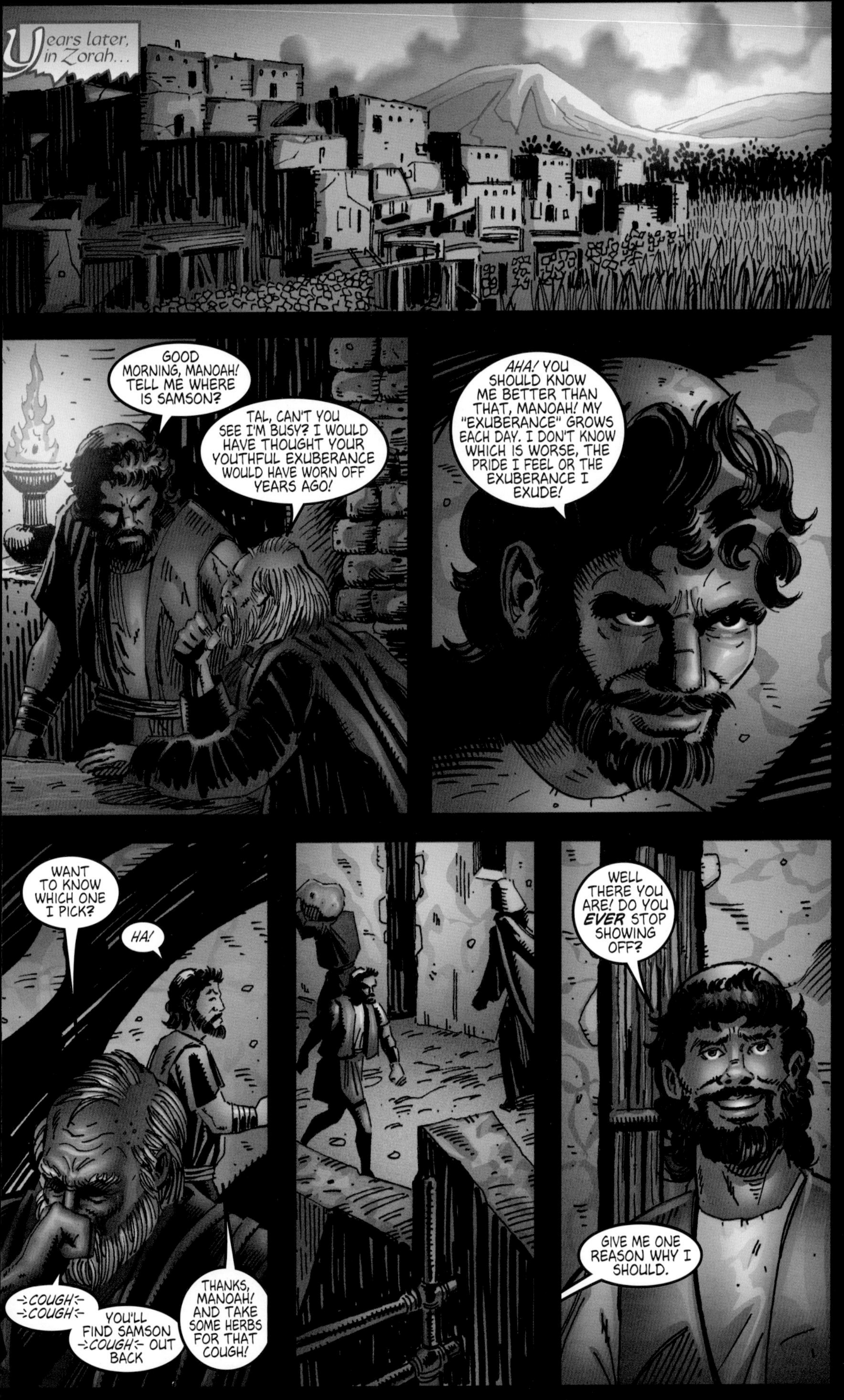
Years later, in Zorah...
GOOD MORNING, MANOAH! TELL ME WHERE IS SAMSON?
TAL, CAN'T YOU SEE I'M BUSY? I WOULD HAVE THOUGHT YOUR YOUTHFUL EXUBERANCE WOULD HAVE WORN OFF YEARS AGO!
AHA! YOU SHOULD KNOW ME BETTER THAN THAT, MANOAH! MY "EXUBERANCE" GROWS EACH DAY. I DON'T KNOW WHICH IS WORSE, THE PRIDE I FEEL OR THE EXUBERANCE I EXUDE!
WANT TO KNOW WHICH ONE I PICK?
HA!
COUGH COUGH
YOU'LL FIND SAMSON COUGH OUT BACK
THANKS, MANOAH! AND TAKE SOME HERBS FOR THAT COUGH!
WELL THERE YOU ARE! DO YOU EVER STOP SHOWING OFF?
GIVE ME ONE REASON WHY I SHOULD.

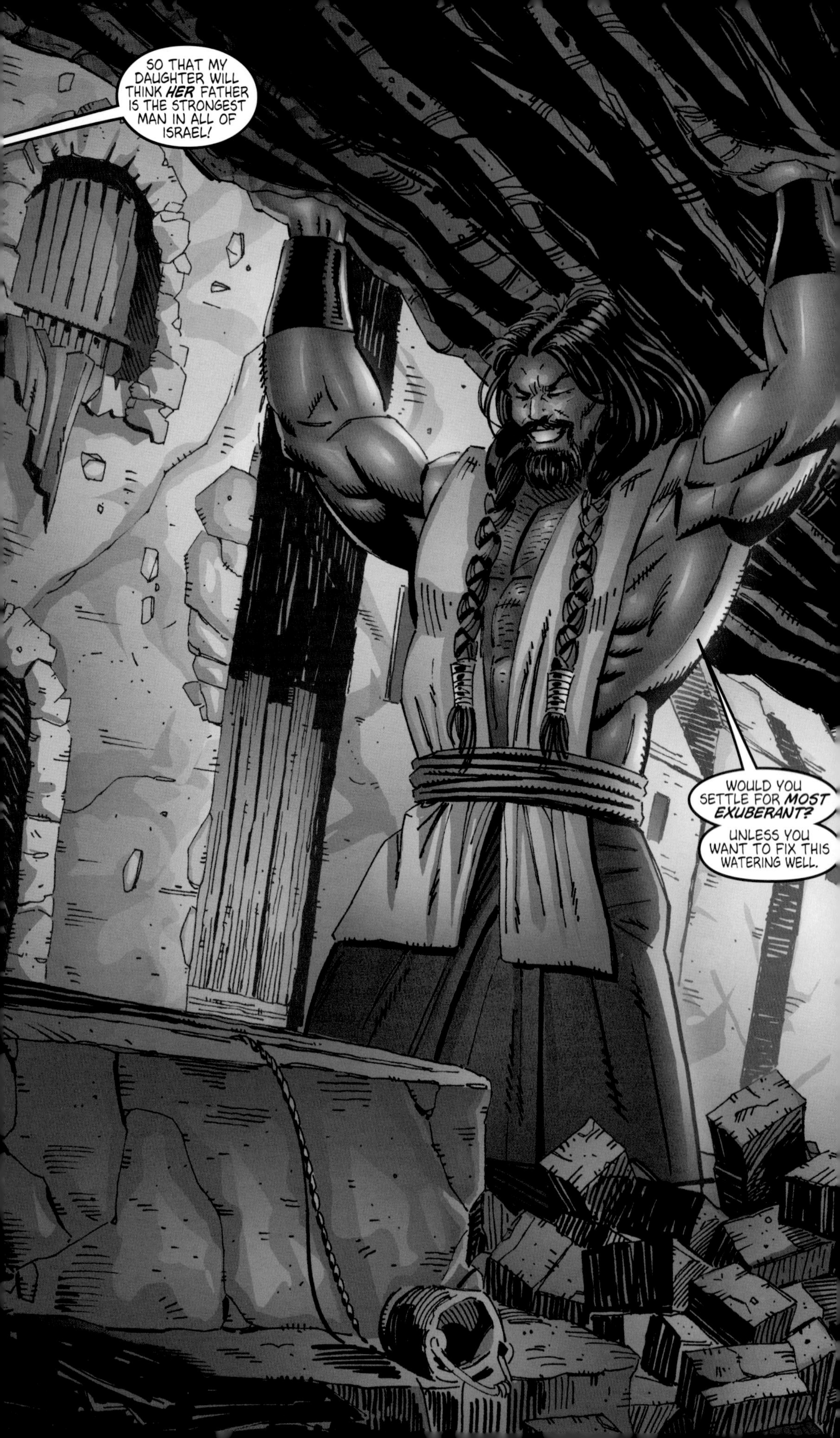
SO THAT MY DAUGHTER WILL THINK **HER** FATHER IS THE STRONGEST MAN IN ALL OF ISRAEL!
WOULD YOU SETTLE FOR ***MOST EXUBERANT?***
UNLESS YOU WANT TO FIX THIS WATERING WELL.

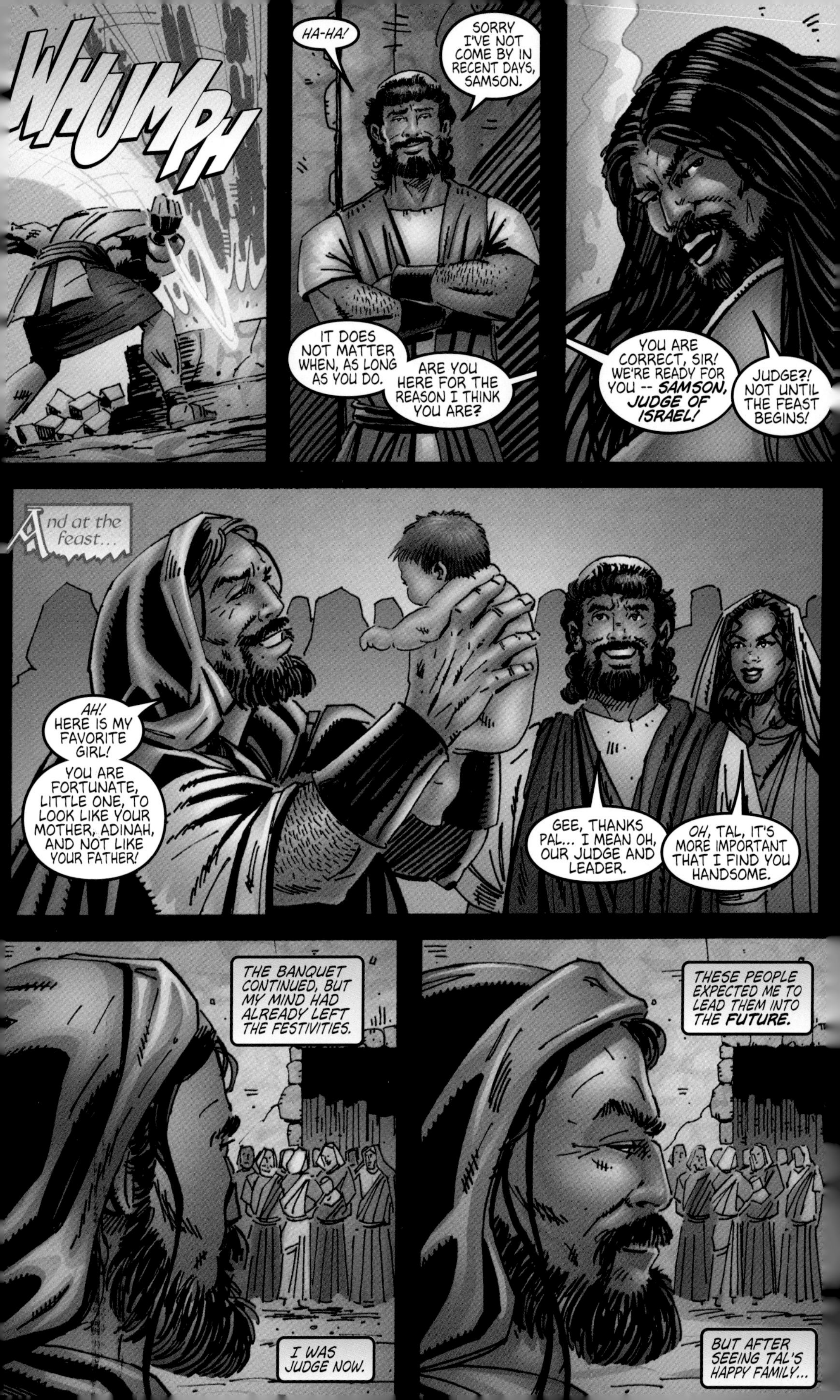
WHUMPH
HA-HA!
SORRY I'VE NOT COME BY IN RECENT DAYS, SAMSON.
IT DOES NOT MATTER WHEN, AS LONG AS YOU DO.
ARE YOU HERE FOR THE REASON I THINK YOU ARE?
YOU ARE CORRECT, SIR! WE'RE READY FOR YOU -- SAMSON, JUDGE OF ISRAEL!
JUDGE?! NOT UNTIL THE FEAST BEGINS!
And at the feast...
AH! HERE IS MY FAVORITE GIRL!
YOU ARE FORTUNATE, LITTLE ONE, TO LOOK LIKE YOUR MOTHER, ADINAH, AND NOT LIKE YOUR FATHER!
GEE, THANKS PAL... I MEAN OH, OUR JUDGE AND LEADER.
OH, TAL, IT'S MORE IMPORTANT THAT I FIND YOU HANDSOME.
THE BANQUET CONTINUED, BUT MY MIND HAD ALREADY LEFT THE FESTIVITIES.
I WAS JUDGE NOW.
THESE PEOPLE EXPECTED ME TO LEAD THEM INTO THE FUTURE.
BUT AFTER SEEING TAL'S HAPPY FAMILY...

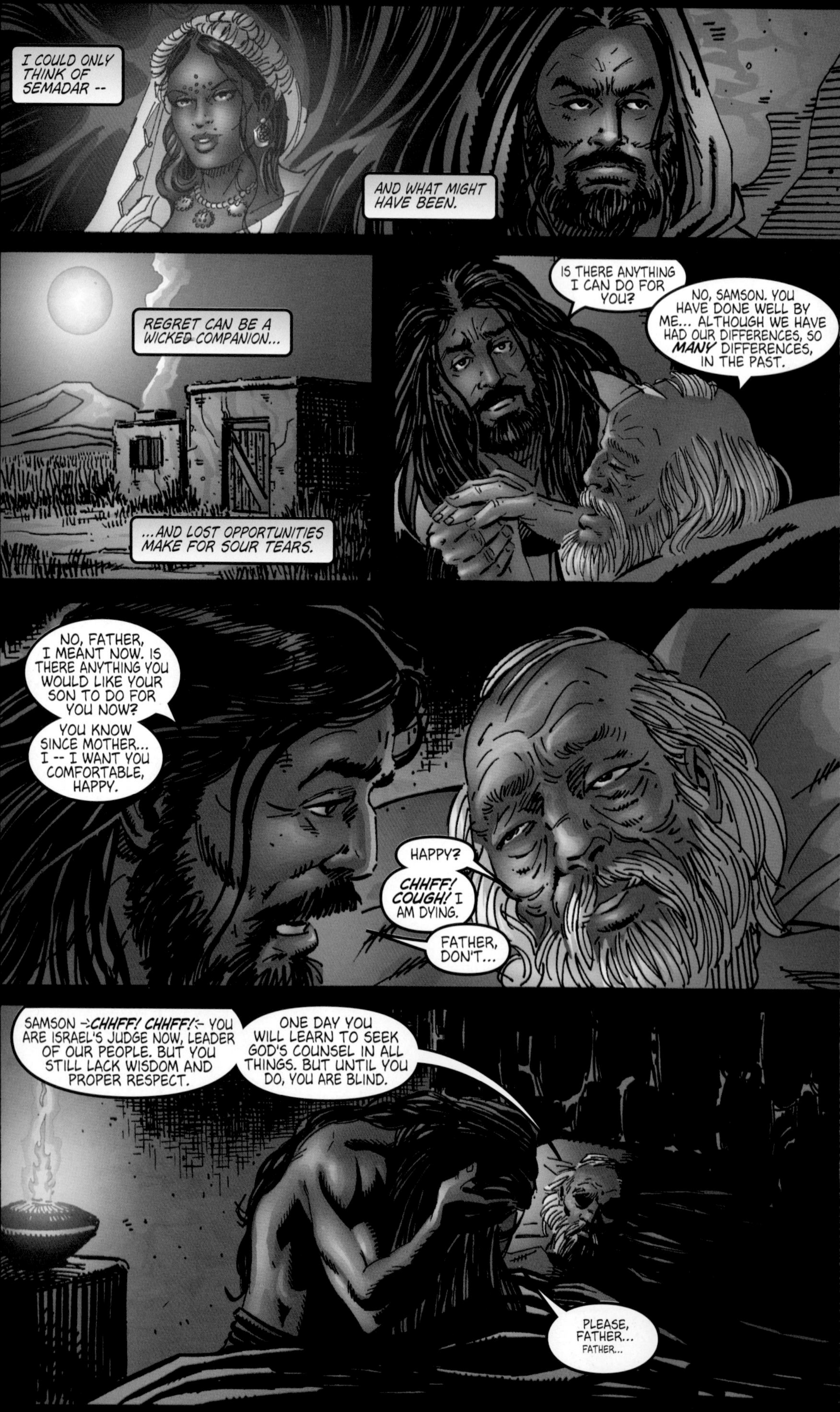
I COULD ONLY THINK OF SEMADAR --
AND WHAT MIGHT HAVE BEEN.
REGRET CAN BE A WICKED COMPANION...
...AND LOST OPPORTUNITIES MAKE FOR SOUR TEARS.
IS THERE ANYTHING I CAN DO FOR YOU?
NO, SAMSON. YOU HAVE DONE WELL BY ME... ALTHOUGH WE HAVE HAD OUR DIFFERENCES, SO *MANY* DIFFERENCES, IN THE PAST.
NO, FATHER, I MEANT NOW. IS THERE ANYTHING YOU WOULD LIKE YOUR SON TO DO FOR YOU NOW?
YOU KNOW SINCE MOTHER... I -- I WANT YOU COMFORTABLE, HAPPY.
HAPPY?
CHHFF! COUGH! I AM DYING.
FATHER, DON'T...
SAMSON -CHHFF! CHHFF!- YOU ARE ISRAEL'S JUDGE NOW, LEADER OF OUR PEOPLE. BUT YOU STILL LACK WISDOM AND PROPER RESPECT.
ONE DAY YOU WILL LEARN TO SEEK GOD'S COUNSEL IN ALL THINGS. BUT UNTIL YOU DO, YOU ARE BLIND.
PLEASE, FATHER... FATHER...

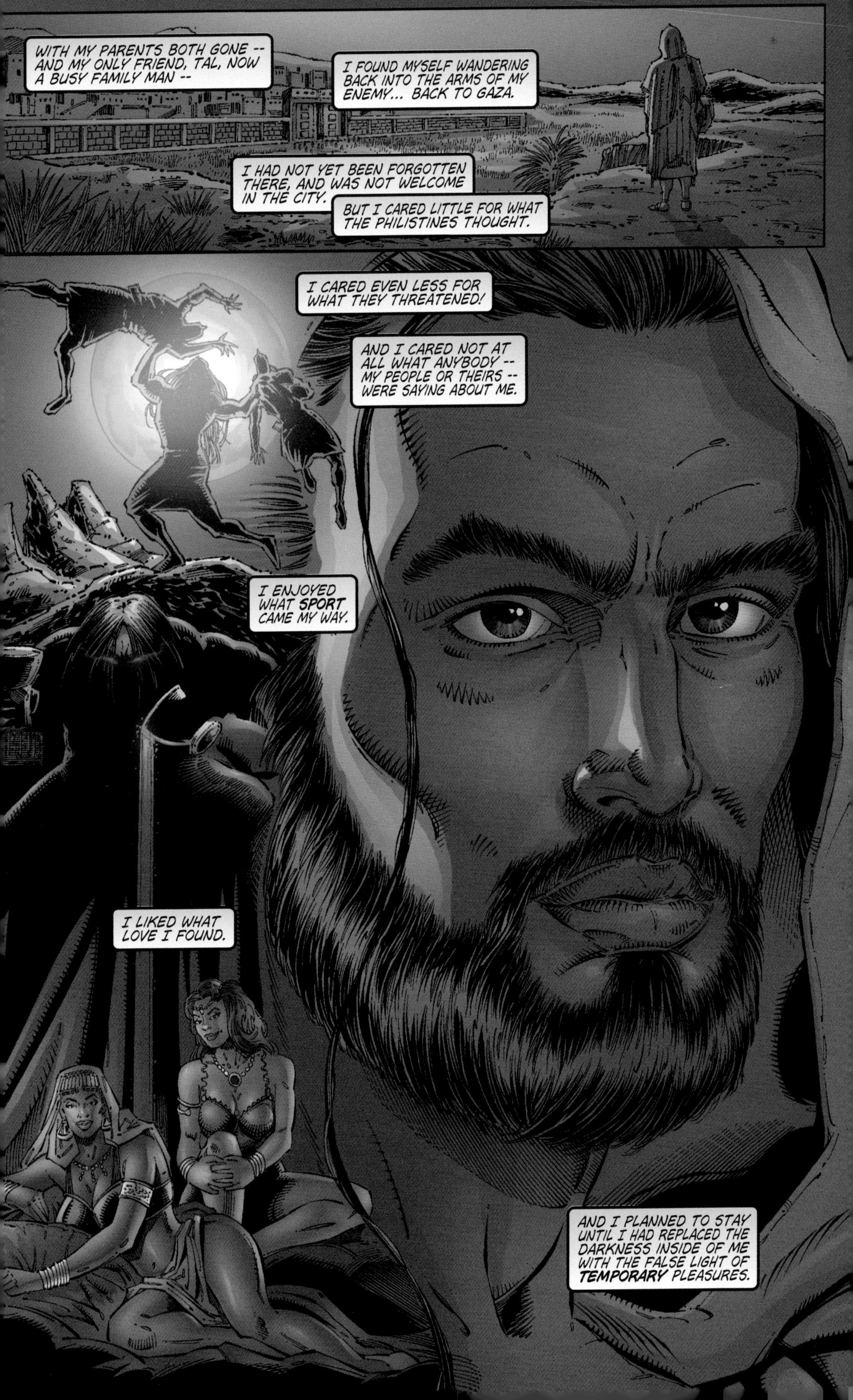
WITH MY PARENTS BOTH GONE -- AND MY ONLY FRIEND, TAL, NOW A BUSY FAMILY MAN --
I FOUND MYSELF WANDERING BACK INTO THE ARMS OF MY ENEMY... BACK TO GAZA.
I HAD NOT YET BEEN FORGOTTEN THERE, AND WAS NOT WELCOME IN THE CITY.
BUT I CARED LITTLE FOR WHAT THE PHILISTINES THOUGHT.
I CARED EVEN LESS FOR WHAT THEY THREATENED!
AND I CARED NOT AT ALL WHAT ANYBODY -- MY PEOPLE OR THEIRS -- WERE SAYING ABOUT ME.
I ENJOYED WHAT **SPORT** CAME MY WAY.
I LIKED WHAT LOVE I FOUND.
AND I PLANNED TO STAY UNTIL I HAD REPLACED THE DARKNESS INSIDE OF ME WITH THE FALSE LIGHT OF **TEMPORARY** PLEASURES.

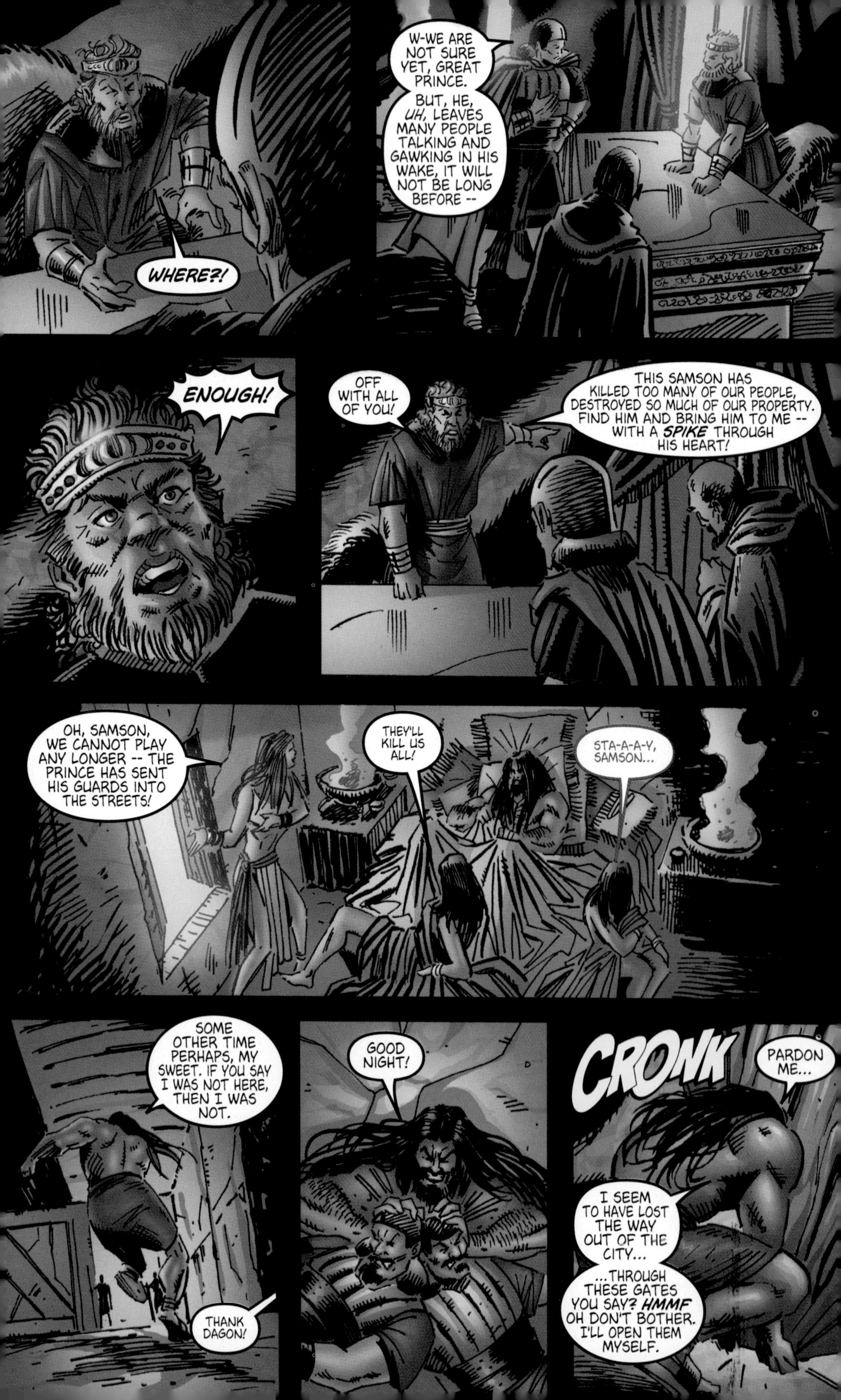
WHERE?!
W-WE ARE NOT SURE YET, GREAT PRINCE.
BUT, HE, UH, LEAVES MANY PEOPLE TALKING AND GAWKING IN HIS WAKE, IT WILL NOT BE LONG BEFORE --
ENOUGH!
OFF WITH ALL OF YOU!
THIS SAMSON HAS KILLED TOO MANY OF OUR PEOPLE, DESTROYED SO MUCH OF OUR PROPERTY. FIND HIM AND BRING HIM TO ME -- WITH A SPIKE THROUGH HIS HEART!
OH, SAMSON, WE CANNOT PLAY ANY LONGER -- THE PRINCE HAS SENT HIS GUARDS INTO THE STREETS!
THEY'LL KILL US ALL!
STA-A-A-Y, SAMSON...
SOME OTHER TIME PERHAPS, MY SWEET. IF YOU SAY I WAS NOT HERE, THEN I WAS NOT.
THANK DAGON!
GOOD NIGHT!
CRONK
PARDON ME...
I SEEM TO HAVE LOST THE WAY OUT OF THE CITY...
...THROUGH THESE GATES YOU SAY? HMMF OH DON'T BOTHER. I'LL OPEN THEM MYSELF.

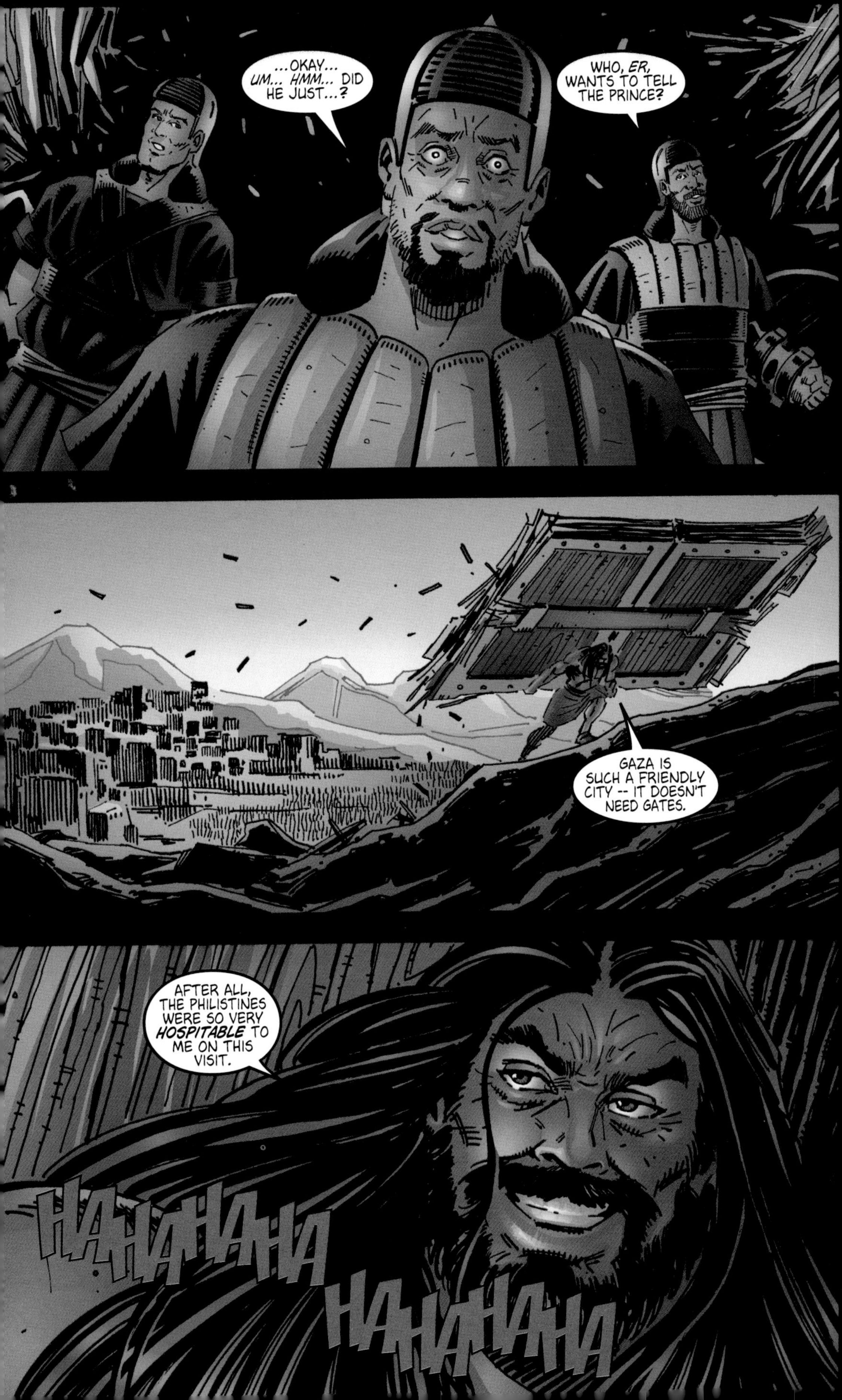
...OKAY... UM... HMM... DID HE JUST...?
WHO, ER, WANTS TO TELL THE PRINCE?
GAZA IS SUCH A FRIENDLY CITY -- IT DOESN'T NEED GATES.
AFTER ALL, THE PHILISTINES WERE SO VERY HOSPITABLE TO ME ON THIS VISIT.
HAHAHAHA
HAHAHAHA

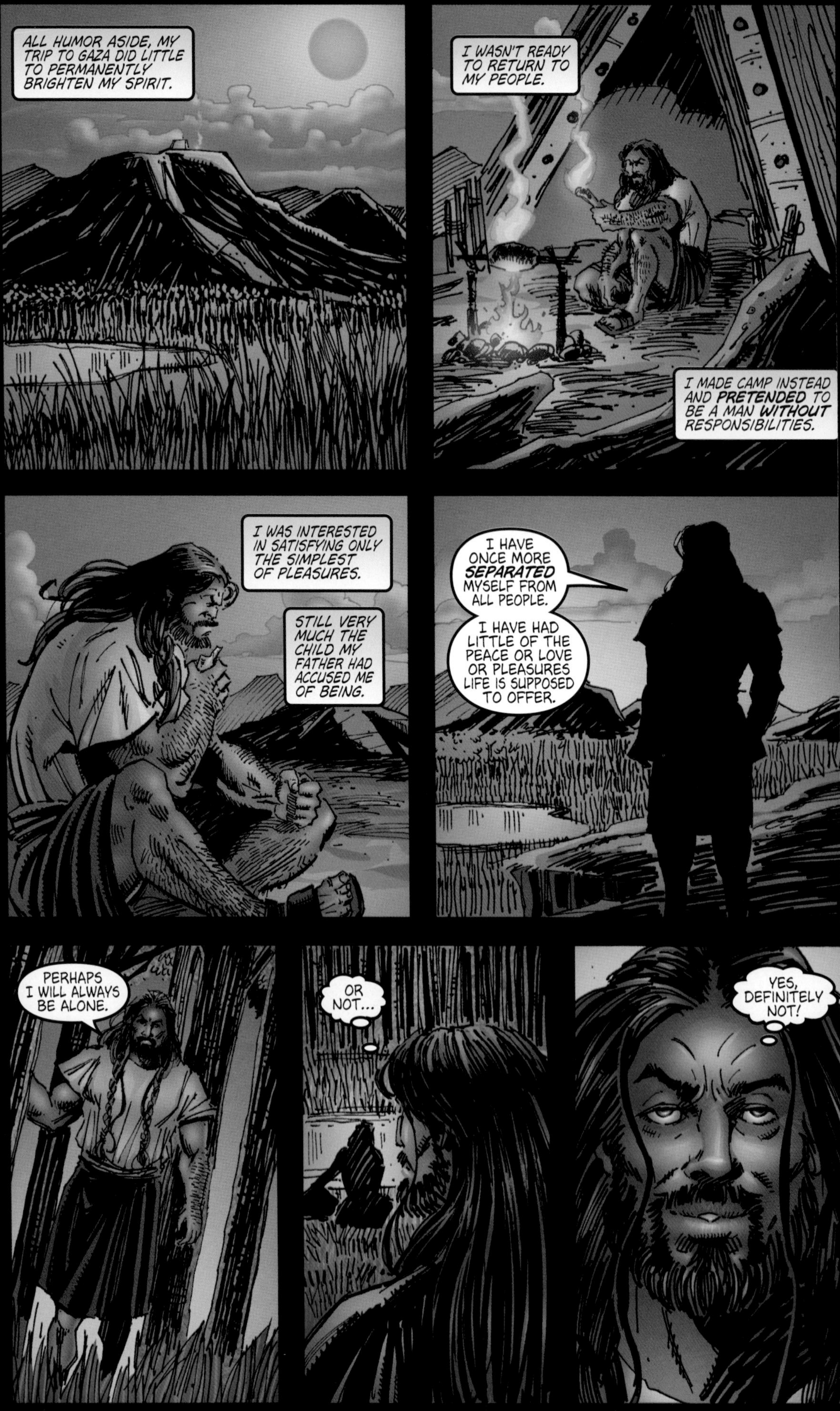
ALL HUMOR ASIDE, MY TRIP TO GAZA DID LITTLE TO PERMANENTLY BRIGHTEN MY SPIRIT.
I WASN'T READY TO RETURN TO MY PEOPLE.
I MADE CAMP INSTEAD AND PRETENDED TO BE A MAN WITHOUT RESPONSIBILITIES.
I WAS INTERESTED IN SATISFYING ONLY THE SIMPLEST OF PLEASURES.
STILL VERY MUCH THE CHILD MY FATHER HAD ACCUSED ME OF BEING.
I HAVE ONCE MORE SEPARATED MYSELF FROM ALL PEOPLE.
I HAVE HAD LITTLE OF THE PEACE OR LOVE OR PLEASURES LIFE IS SUPPOSED TO OFFER.
PERHAPS I WILL ALWAYS BE ALONE.
OR NOT...
YES, DEFINITELY NOT!

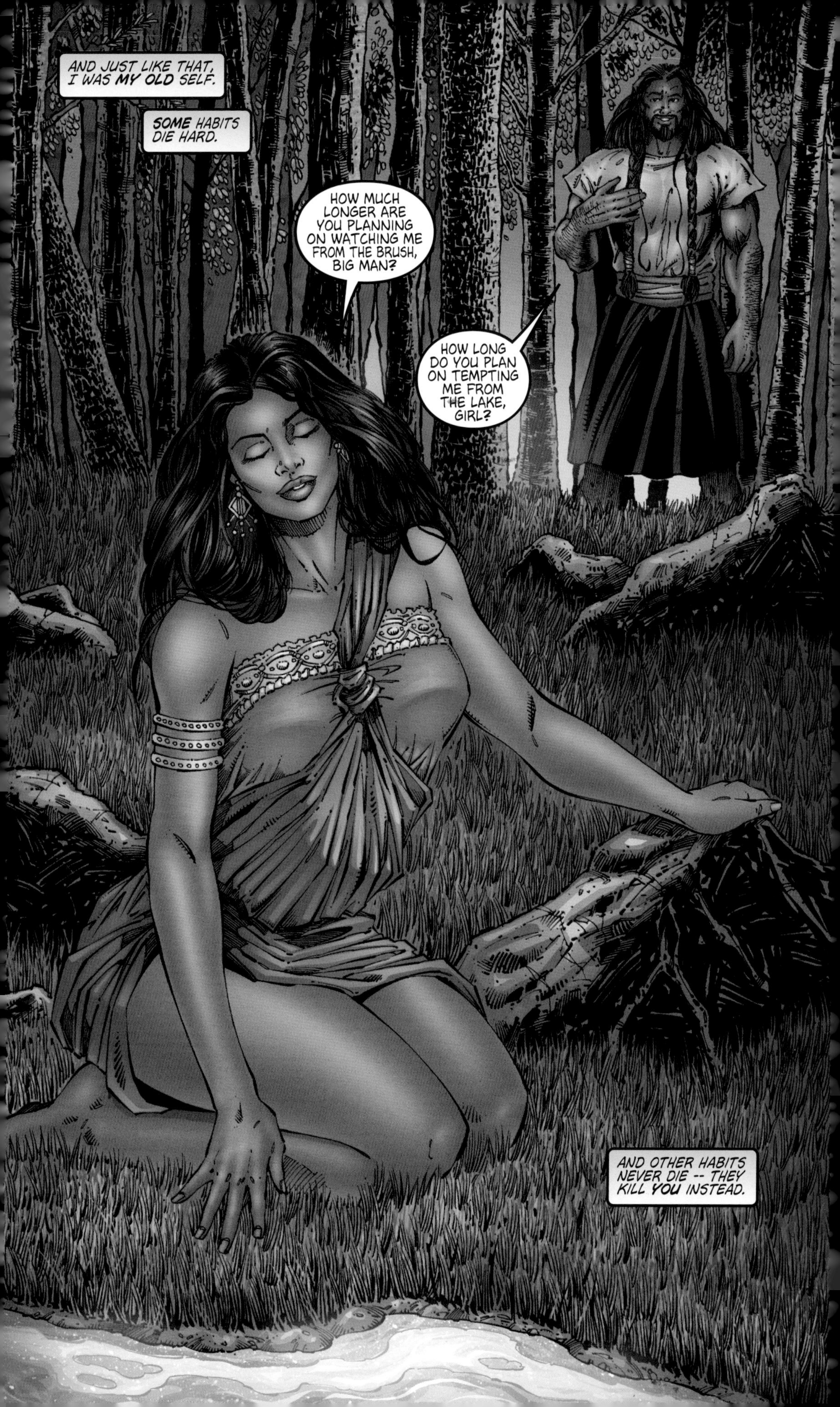
AND JUST LIKE THAT, I WAS MY OLD SELF.
SOME HABITS DIE HARD.
HOW MUCH LONGER ARE YOU PLANNING ON WATCHING ME FROM THE BRUSH, BIG MAN?
HOW LONG DO YOU PLAN ON TEMPTING ME FROM THE LAKE, GIRL?
AND OTHER HABITS NEVER DIE -- THEY KILL YOU INSTEAD.

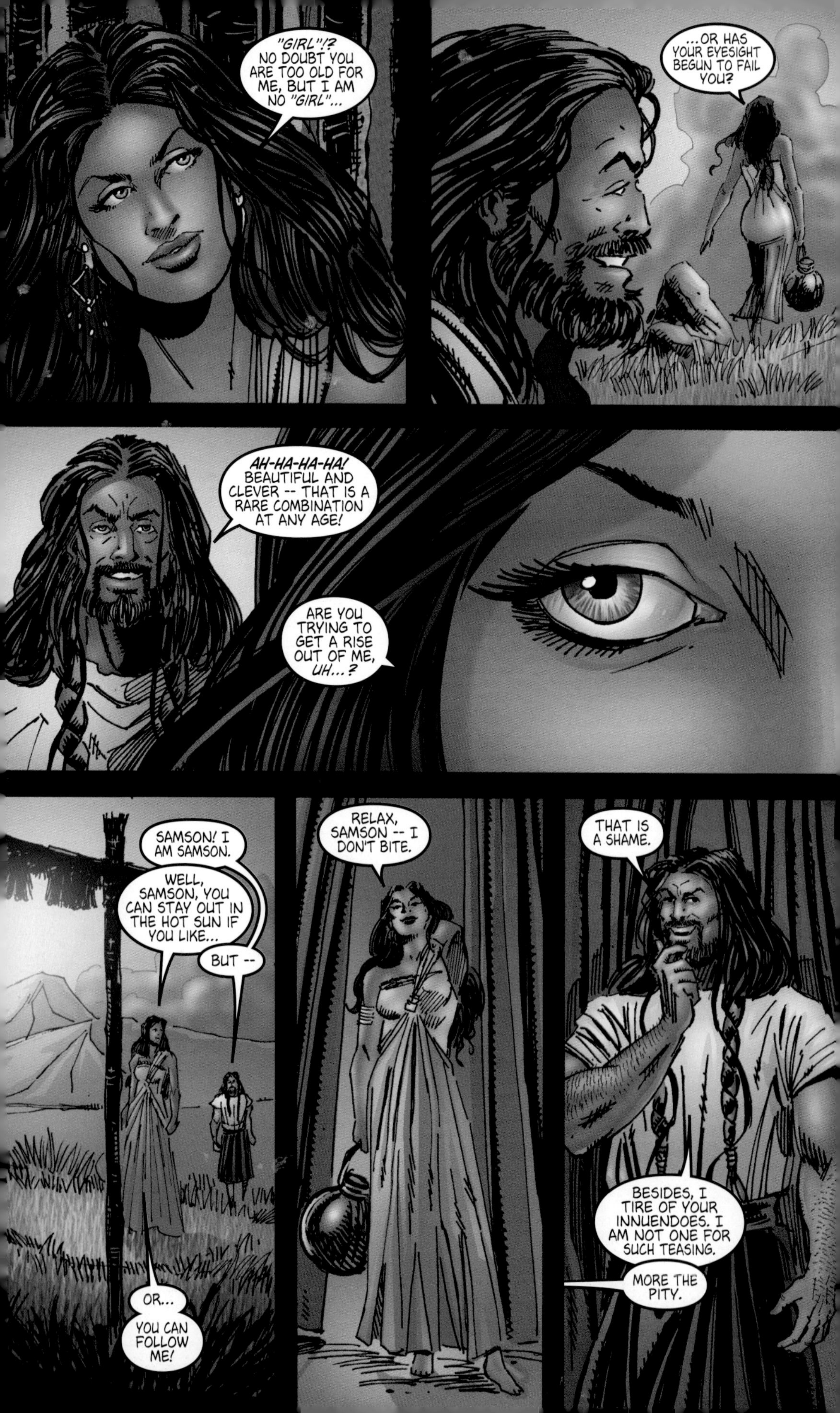
"GIRL"!? NO DOUBT YOU ARE TOO OLD FOR ME, BUT I AM NO "GIRL"...
...OR HAS YOUR EYESIGHT BEGUN TO FAIL YOU?
AH-HA-HA-HA! BEAUTIFUL AND CLEVER -- THAT IS A RARE COMBINATION AT ANY AGE!
ARE YOU TRYING TO GET A RISE OUT OF ME, UH...?
SAMSON! I AM SAMSON.
WELL, SAMSON, YOU CAN STAY OUT IN THE HOT SUN IF YOU LIKE...
BUT --
OR...
YOU CAN FOLLOW ME!
RELAX, SAMSON -- I DON'T BITE.
THAT IS A SHAME.
BESIDES, I TIRE OF YOUR INNUENDOES. I AM NOT ONE FOR SUCH TEASING.
MORE THE PITY.

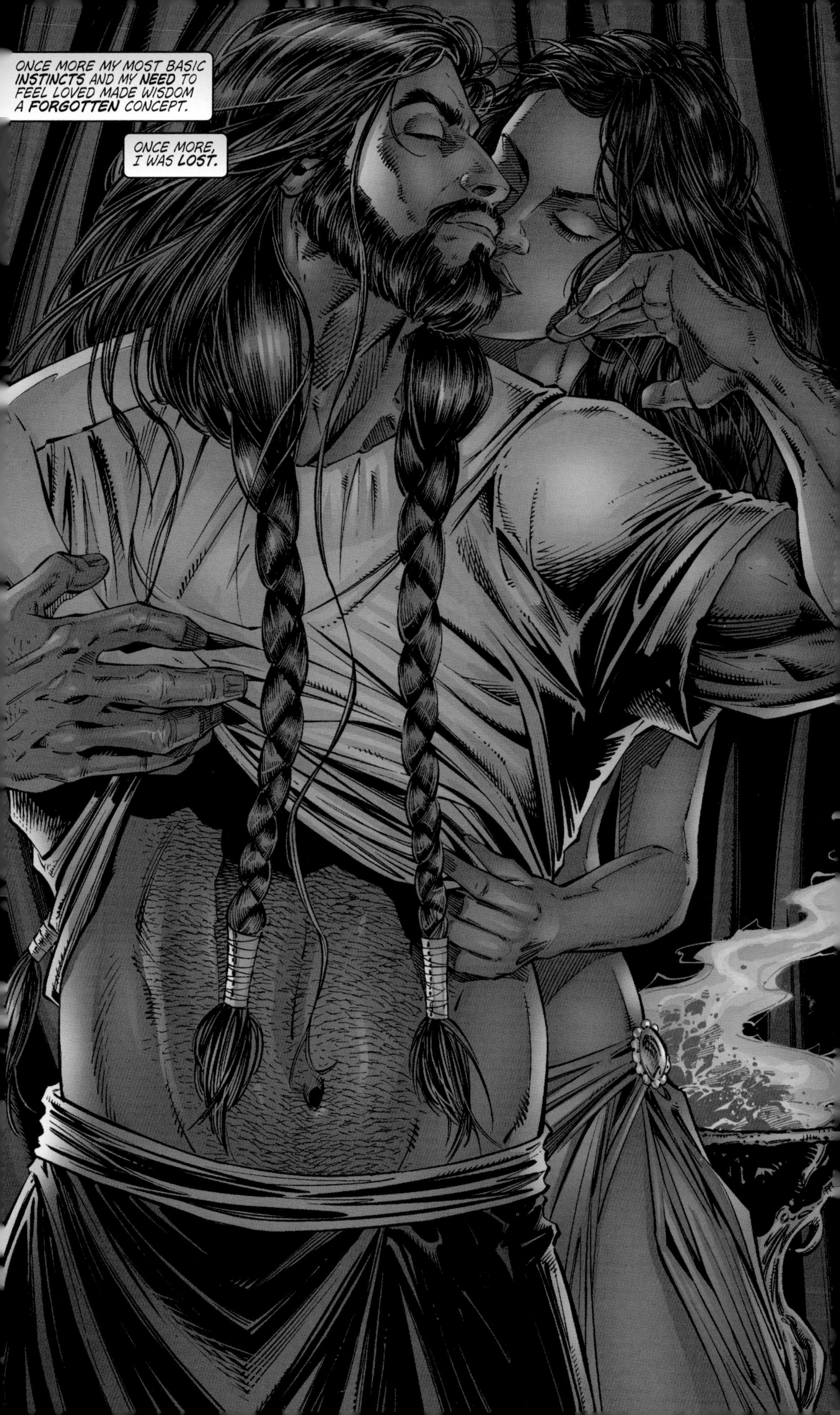
ONCE MORE MY MOST BASIC INSTINCTS AND MY NEED TO FEEL LOVED MADE WISDOM A FORGOTTEN CONCEPT.
ONCE MORE, I WAS LOST.

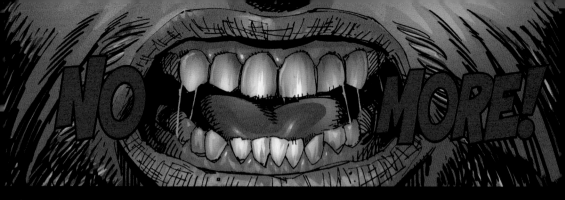

NO MORE!

THIS MAN DEFILES OUR GOD AND THEN LAUGHS AT US! HE WALKS INTO THE DESERT AND YOU CANNOT FIND HIM IN A SEA OF SAND!

THIS CANNOT CONTINUE... I CANNOT --

YOUR EXCELLENCE... WE DO --

ON YOUR LIFE, YOU HAD BETTER BE INTERRUPTING ME FOR A *VERY* GOOD REASON!

WE ARE, MY PRINCE...

YOU SEE, WE DID HEAR WORD OF HIS PRESENCE -- IN SOREK.

YES, YES... AND, *UH*, HE COMES AND GOES, AT WILL... H-HE TRAVELS FAR FOR FOOD BUT ALWAYS RETURNS.

RETURNS? FOR *WHAT*?!

FOR *HER*, MY PRINCE!

...FOR HER!

GOOD DAY, PRINCE *TANEK*... IF I MIGHT BE GRANTED A FEW MOMENTS -- I THINK WE COULD MAKE EACH OTHER VERY, VERY HAPPY!

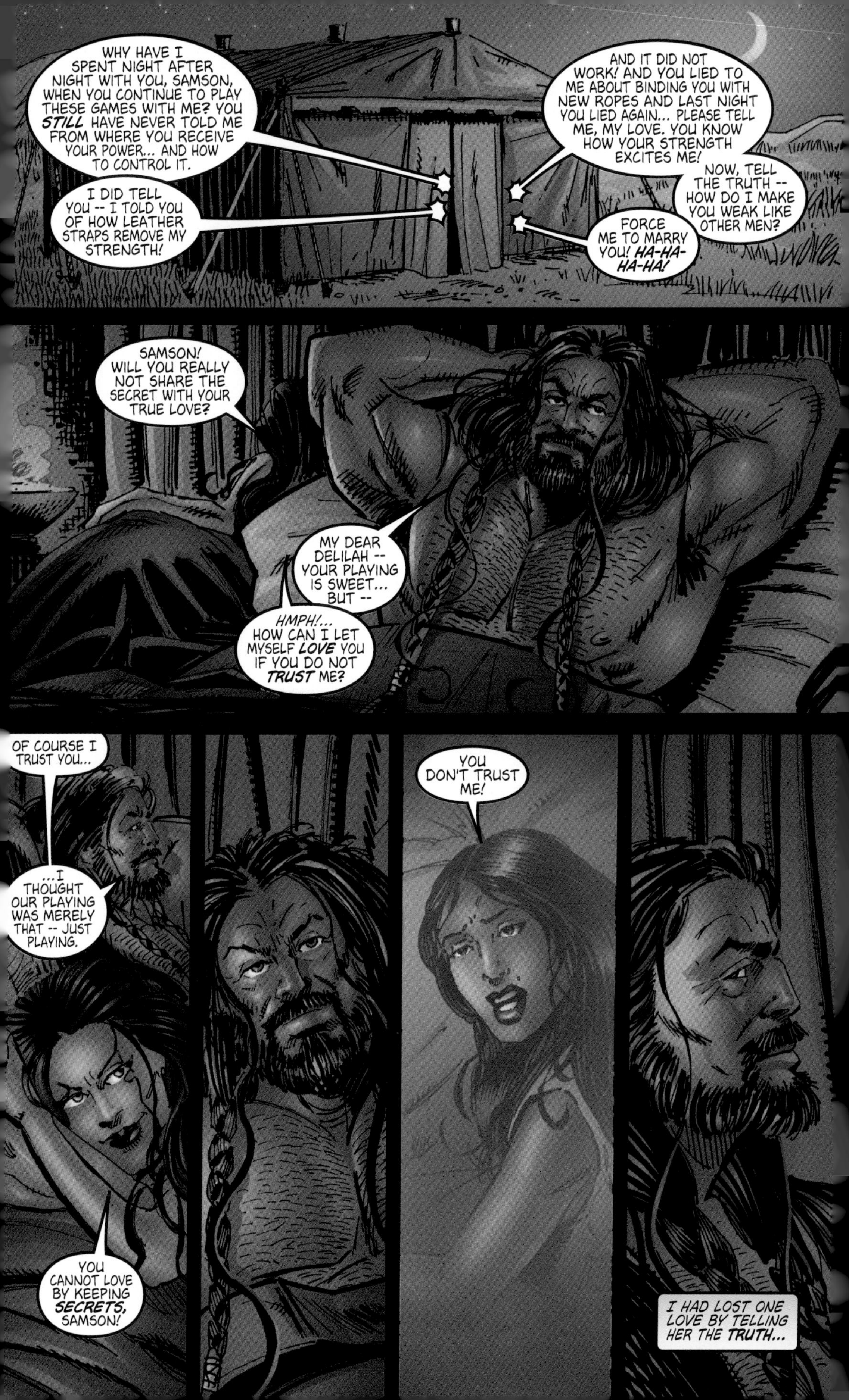
WHY HAVE I SPENT NIGHT AFTER NIGHT WITH YOU, SAMSON, WHEN YOU CONTINUE TO PLAY THESE GAMES WITH ME? YOU STILL HAVE NEVER TOLD ME FROM WHERE YOU RECEIVE YOUR POWER... AND HOW TO CONTROL IT.
I DID TELL YOU -- I TOLD YOU OF HOW LEATHER STRAPS REMOVE MY STRENGTH!
AND IT DID NOT WORK! AND YOU LIED TO ME ABOUT BINDING YOU WITH NEW ROPES AND LAST NIGHT YOU LIED AGAIN... PLEASE TELL ME, MY LOVE. YOU KNOW HOW YOUR STRENGTH EXCITES ME!
NOW, TELL THE TRUTH -- HOW DO I MAKE YOU WEAK LIKE OTHER MEN?
FORCE ME TO MARRY YOU! HA-HA-HA-HA!
SAMSON! WILL YOU REALLY NOT SHARE THE SECRET WITH YOUR TRUE LOVE?
MY DEAR DELILAH -- YOUR PLAYING IS SWEET... BUT --
HMPH!... HOW CAN I LET MYSELF LOVE YOU IF YOU DO NOT TRUST ME?
OF COURSE I TRUST YOU...
...I THOUGHT OUR PLAYING WAS MERELY THAT -- JUST PLAYING.
YOU CANNOT LOVE BY KEEPING SECRETS, SAMSON!
YOU DON'T TRUST ME!
I HAD LOST ONE LOVE BY TELLING HER THE TRUTH...

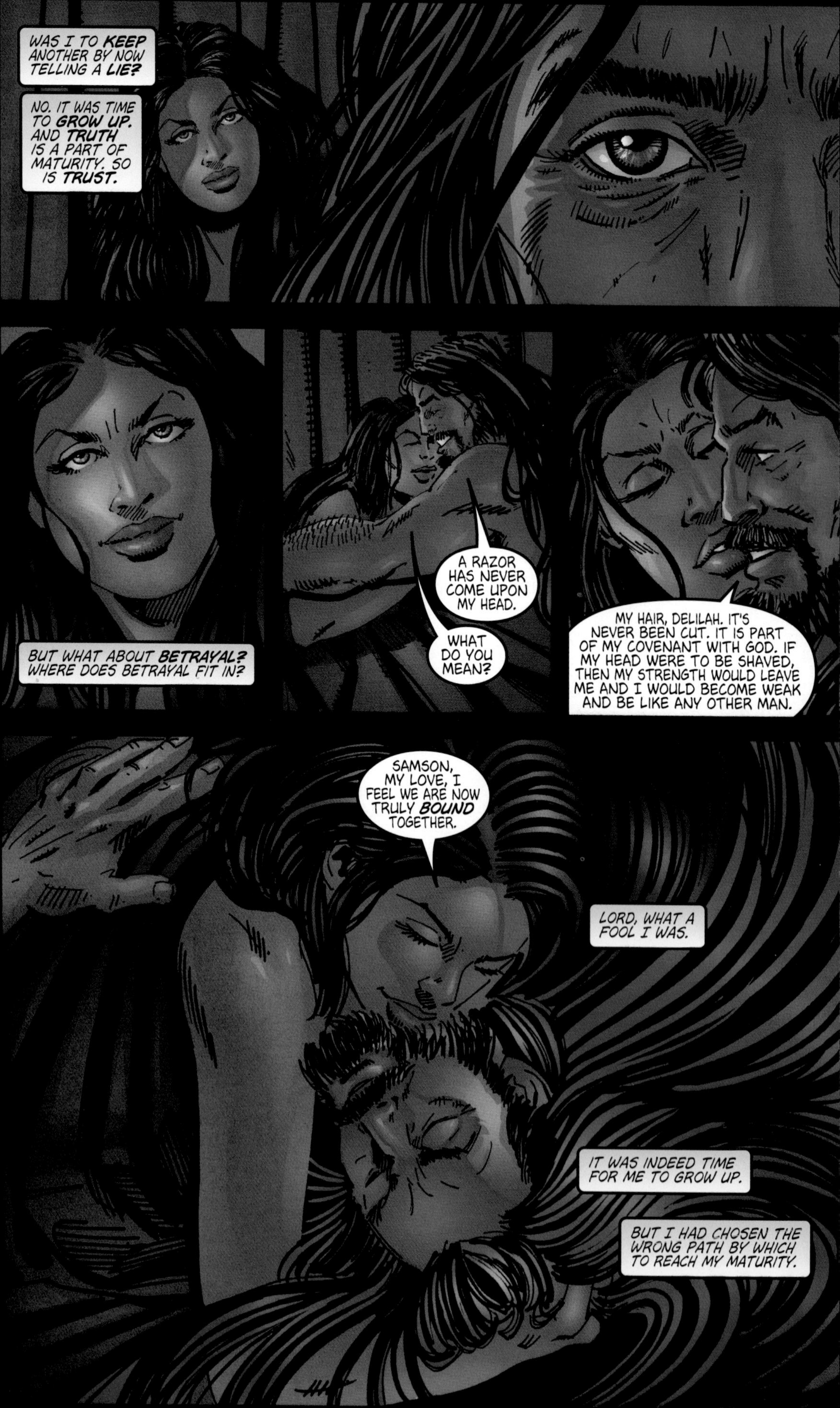

WAS I TO **KEEP** ANOTHER BY NOW TELLING A **LIE?**
NO. IT WAS TIME TO **GROW UP.** AND **TRUTH** IS A PART OF MATURITY. SO IS **TRUST.**
BUT WHAT ABOUT **BETRAYAL?** WHERE DOES BETRAYAL FIT IN?
A RAZOR HAS NEVER COME UPON MY HEAD.
WHAT DO YOU MEAN?
MY HAIR, DELILAH. IT'S NEVER BEEN CUT. IT IS PART OF MY COVENANT WITH GOD. IF MY HEAD WERE TO BE SHAVED, THEN MY STRENGTH WOULD LEAVE ME AND I WOULD BECOME WEAK AND BE LIKE ANY OTHER MAN.
SAMSON, MY LOVE, I FEEL WE ARE NOW TRULY **BOUND** TOGETHER.
LORD, WHAT A FOOL I WAS.
IT WAS INDEED TIME FOR ME TO GROW UP.
BUT I HAD CHOSEN THE WRONG PATH BY WHICH TO REACH MY MATURITY.

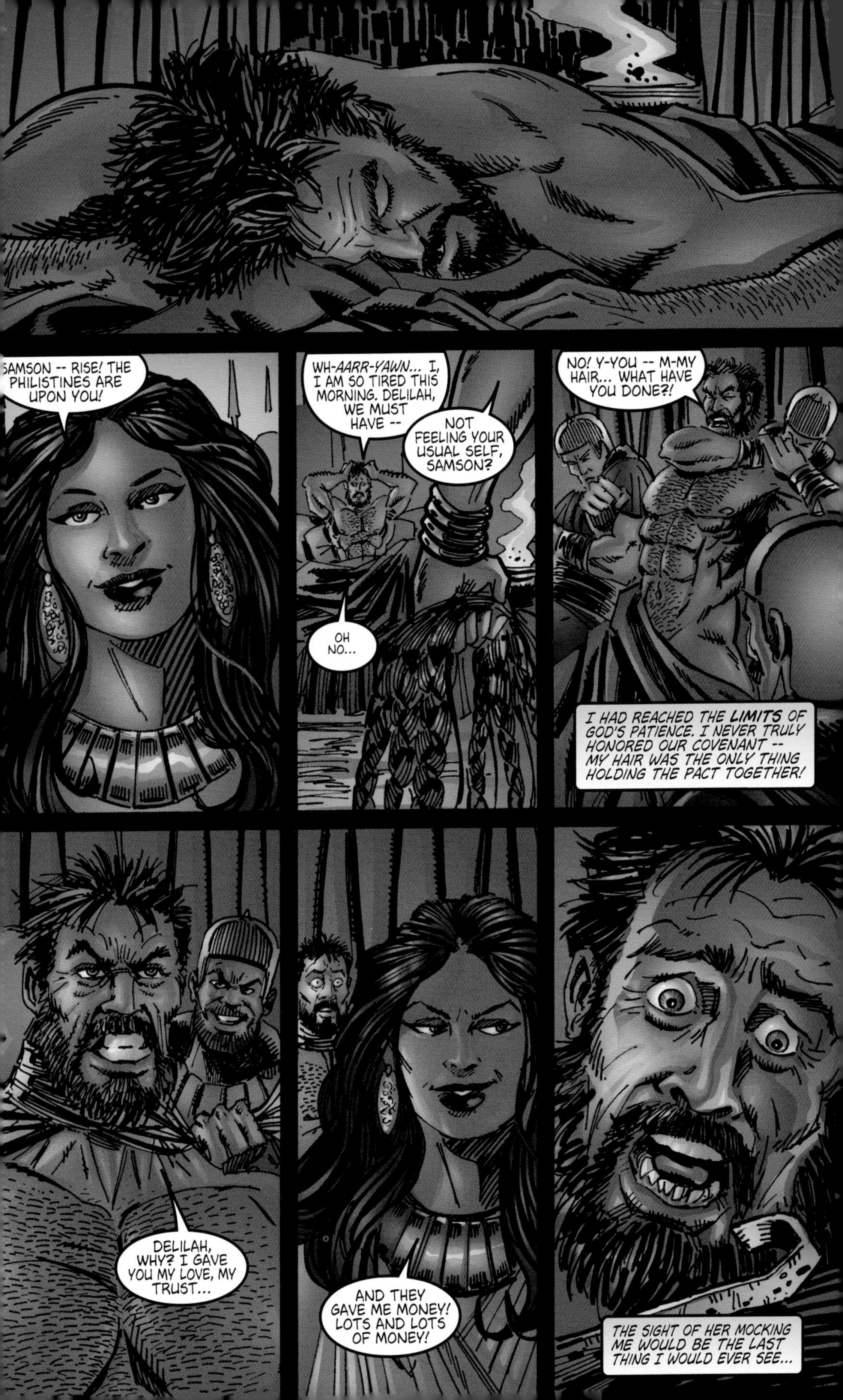
SAMSON -- RISE! THE PHILISTINES ARE UPON YOU!
WH-AARR-YAWN... I, I AM SO TIRED THIS MORNING. DELILAH, WE MUST HAVE --
NOT FEELING YOUR USUAL SELF, SAMSON?
OH NO...
NO! Y-YOU -- M-MY HAIR... WHAT HAVE YOU DONE?!
I HAD REACHED THE LIMITS OF GOD'S PATIENCE. I NEVER TRULY HONORED OUR COVENANT -- MY HAIR WAS THE ONLY THING HOLDING THE PACT TOGETHER!
DELILAH, WHY? I GAVE YOU MY LOVE, MY TRUST...
AND THEY GAVE ME MONEY! LOTS AND LOTS OF MONEY!
THE SIGHT OF HER MOCKING ME WOULD BE THE LAST THING I WOULD EVER SEE...

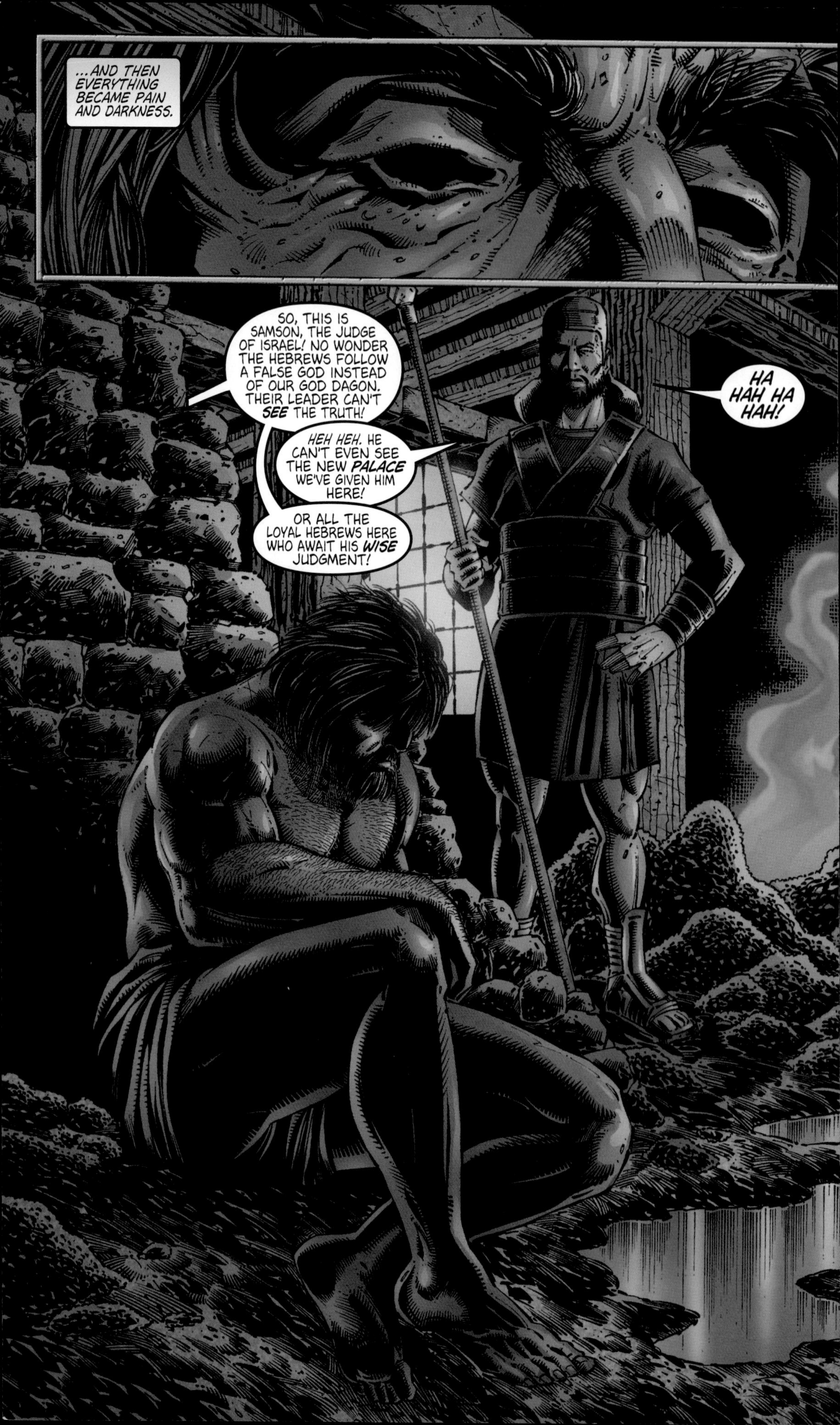
...AND THEN EVERYTHING BECAME PAIN AND DARKNESS.
SO, THIS IS SAMSON, THE JUDGE OF ISRAEL! NO WONDER THE HEBREWS FOLLOW A FALSE GOD INSTEAD OF OUR GOD DAGON. THEIR LEADER CAN'T SEE THE TRUTH!
OR ALL THE LOYAL HEBREWS HERE WHO AWAIT HIS WISE JUDGMENT!
HEH HEH. HE CAN'T EVEN SEE THE NEW PALACE WE'VE GIVEN HIM HERE!
HA HAH HA HAH!

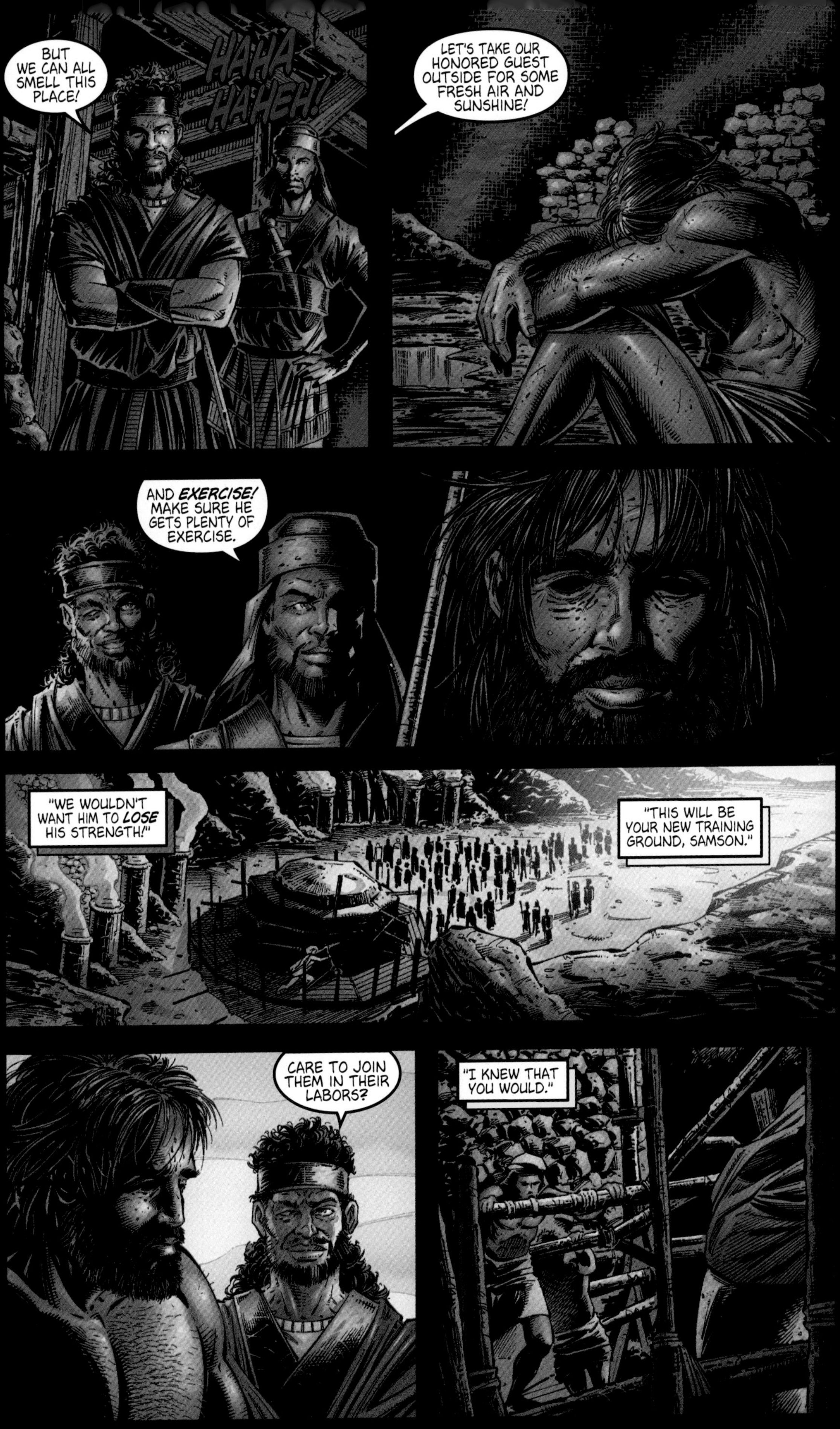
BUT WE CAN ALL SMELL THIS PLACE!
HAHA HAHEH!
LET'S TAKE OUR HONORED GUEST OUTSIDE FOR SOME FRESH AIR AND SUNSHINE!
AND EXERCISE! MAKE SURE HE GETS PLENTY OF EXERCISE.
"WE WOULDN'T WANT HIM TO LOSE HIS STRENGTH!"
"THIS WILL BE YOUR NEW TRAINING GROUND, SAMSON."
CARE TO JOIN THEM IN THEIR LABORS?
"I KNEW THAT YOU WOULD."

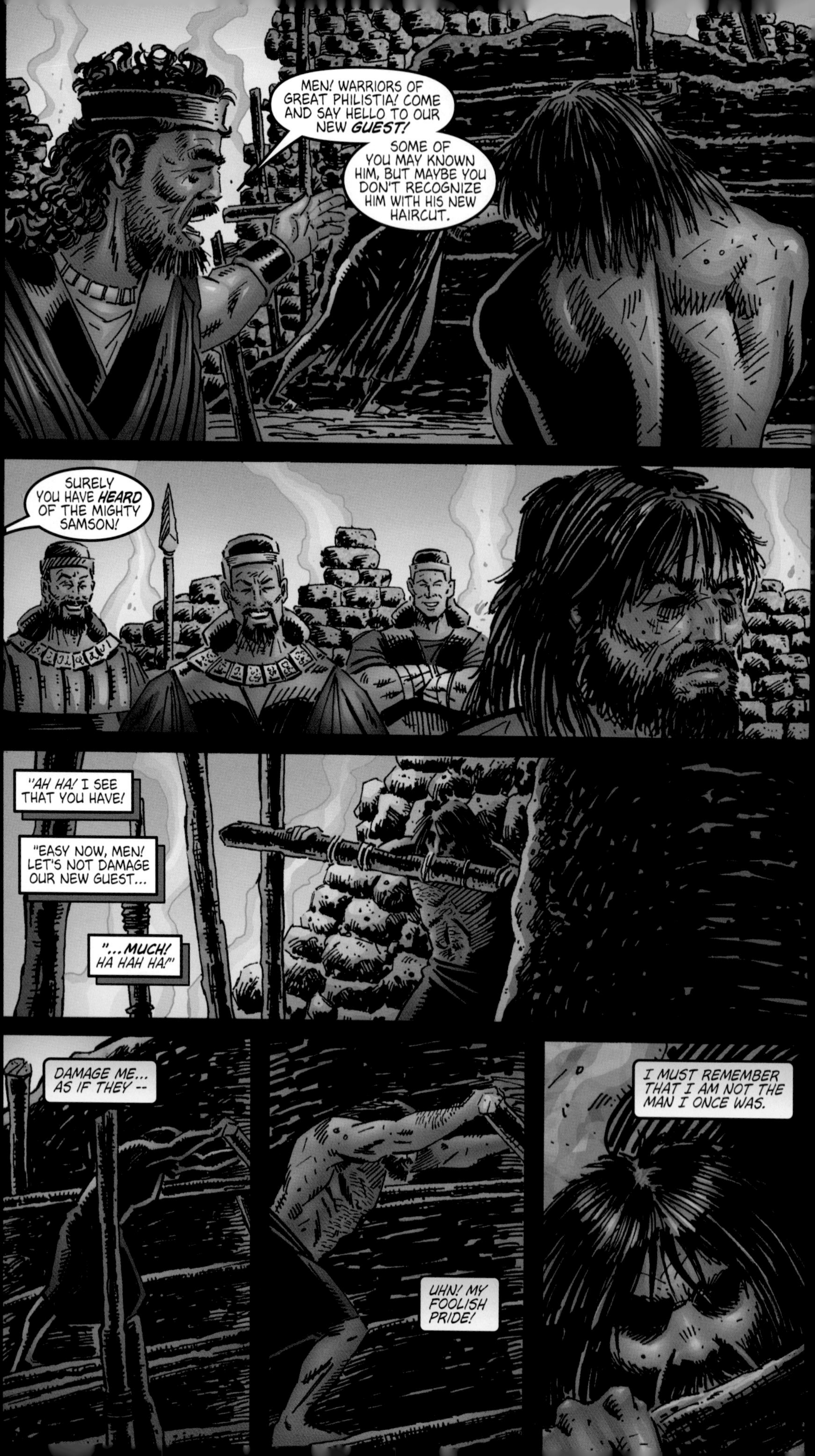
MEN! WARRIORS OF GREAT PHILISTIA! COME AND SAY HELLO TO OUR NEW GUEST!
SOME OF YOU MAY KNOWN HIM, BUT MAYBE YOU DON'T RECOGNIZE HIM WITH HIS NEW HAIRCUT.
SURELY YOU HAVE HEARD OF THE MIGHTY SAMSON!
"AH HA! I SEE THAT YOU HAVE!
"EASY NOW, MEN! LET'S NOT DAMAGE OUR NEW GUEST...
"...MUCH! HA HAH HA!"
DAMAGE ME... AS IF THEY --
UHN! MY FOOLISH PRIDE!
I MUST REMEMBER THAT I AM NOT THE MAN I ONCE WAS.

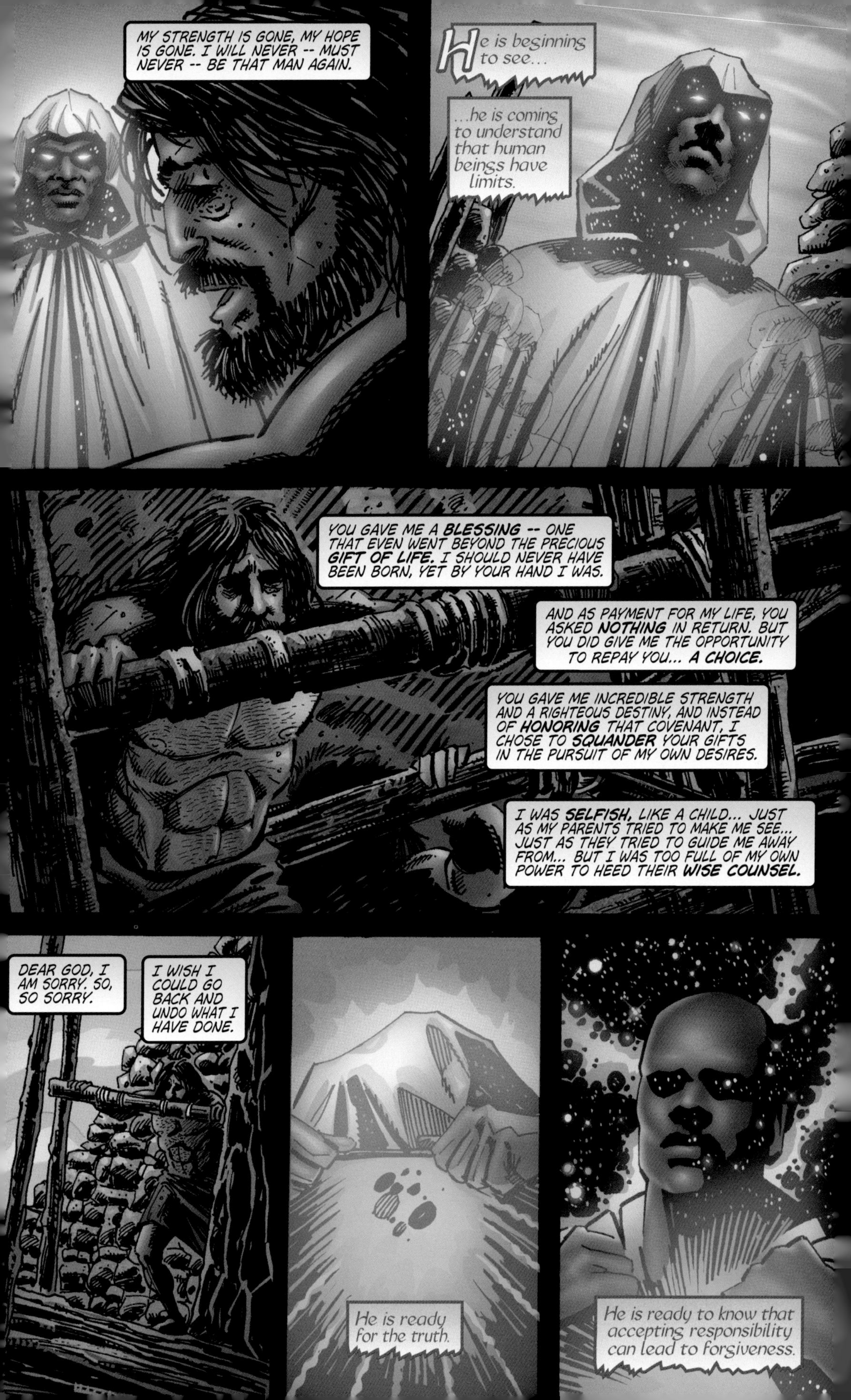
MY STRENGTH IS GONE, MY HOPE IS GONE. I WILL NEVER -- MUST NEVER -- BE THAT MAN AGAIN.
He is beginning to see...
...he is coming to understand that human beings have limits.
YOU GAVE ME A BLESSING -- ONE THAT EVEN WENT BEYOND THE PRECIOUS GIFT OF LIFE. I SHOULD NEVER HAVE BEEN BORN, YET BY YOUR HAND I WAS.
AND AS PAYMENT FOR MY LIFE, YOU ASKED NOTHING IN RETURN. BUT YOU DID GIVE ME THE OPPORTUNITY TO REPAY YOU... A CHOICE.
YOU GAVE ME INCREDIBLE STRENGTH AND A RIGHTEOUS DESTINY, AND INSTEAD OF HONORING THAT COVENANT, I CHOSE TO SQUANDER YOUR GIFTS IN THE PURSUIT OF MY OWN DESIRES.
I WAS SELFISH, LIKE A CHILD... JUST AS MY PARENTS TRIED TO MAKE ME SEE... JUST AS THEY TRIED TO GUIDE ME AWAY FROM... BUT I WAS TOO FULL OF MY OWN POWER TO HEED THEIR WISE COUNSEL.
DEAR GOD, I AM SORRY. SO, SO SORRY.
I WISH I COULD GO BACK AND UNDO WHAT I HAVE DONE.
He is ready for the truth.
He is ready to know that accepting responsibility can lead to forgiveness.

LORD GOD, GOD OF MY FATHERS! I CANNOT GO BACK!
I CANNOT GO BACK...
SO WHAT CAN I DO, FATHER GOD? HOW CAN I APOLOGIZE FOR BREAKING OUR COVENANT, FOR WASTING THE LIFE YOU HAVE GIVEN ME? WHAT CAN I DO TO ATONE FOR THE DAMAGE I'VE DONE?
YOU MADE ME STRONG, TO BE JUDGE OVER YOUR PEOPLE -- **A LEADER --** AND HERE THEY ARE... HERE I AM... IN BONDAGE.
CAN YOU **EVER FORGIVE** ME? COULD YOU?
I AM SPENT... EMPTY INSIDE...
...AND YET SUDDENLY I FEEL A SPARK. IS THIS FROM YOU, LORD? IS THIS YOUR FORGIVENESS? COULD IT BE THAT SIMPLE?
I ASK AND **YOU FORGIVE?** I SEE BEYOND MY BLINDNESS AND YOU MEET ME WITH LOVING ARMS WIDE OPEN?

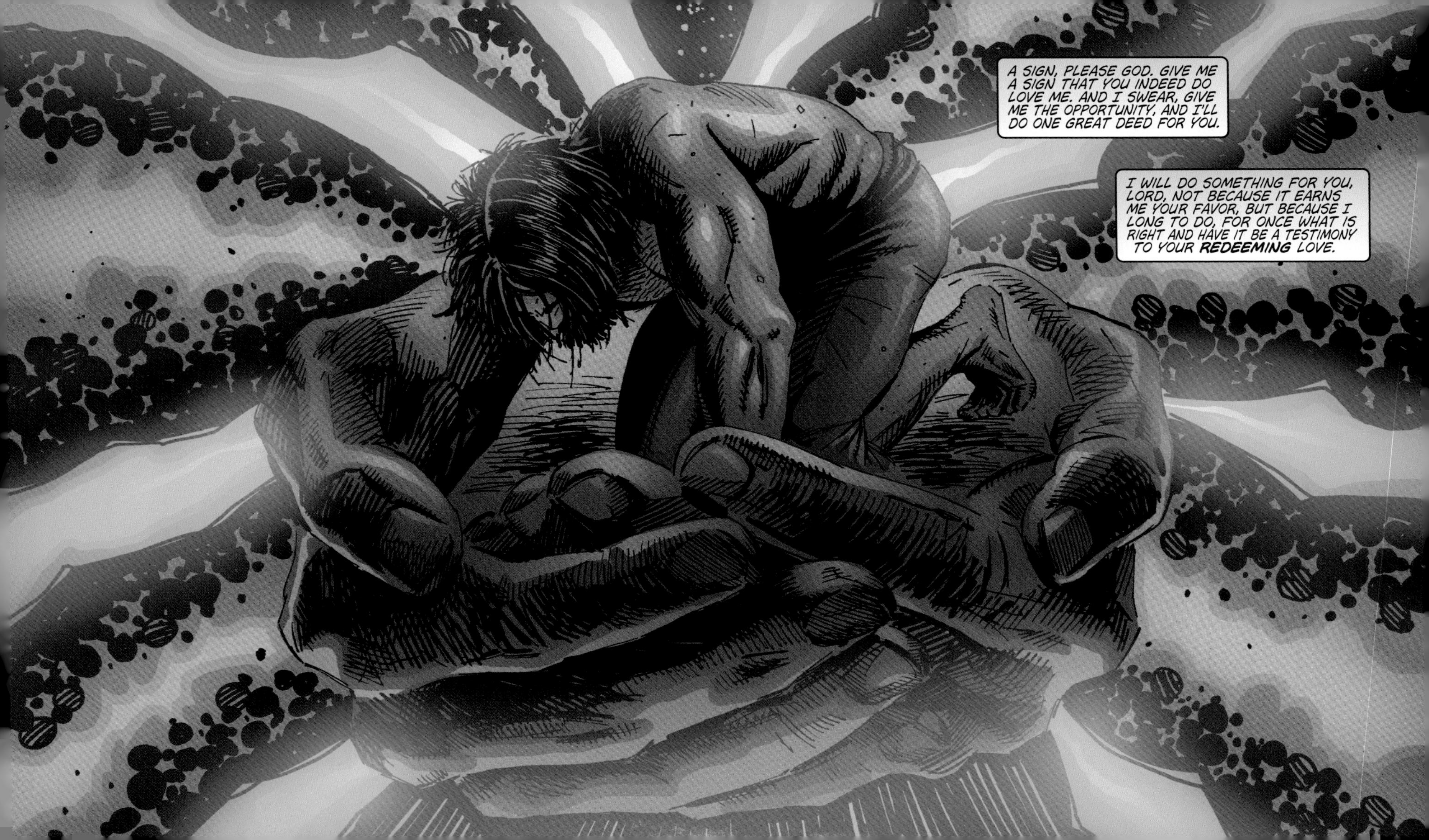
A SIGN, PLEASE GOD. GIVE ME A SIGN THAT YOU INDEED DO LOVE ME. AND I SWEAR, GIVE ME THE OPPORTUNITY, AND I'LL DO ONE GREAT DEED FOR YOU.
I WILL DO SOMETHING FOR YOU, LORD, NOT BECAUSE IT EARNS ME YOUR FAVOR, BUT BECAUSE I LONG TO DO, FOR ONCE WHAT IS RIGHT AND HAVE IT BE A TESTIMONY TO YOUR **REDEEMING** LOVE.

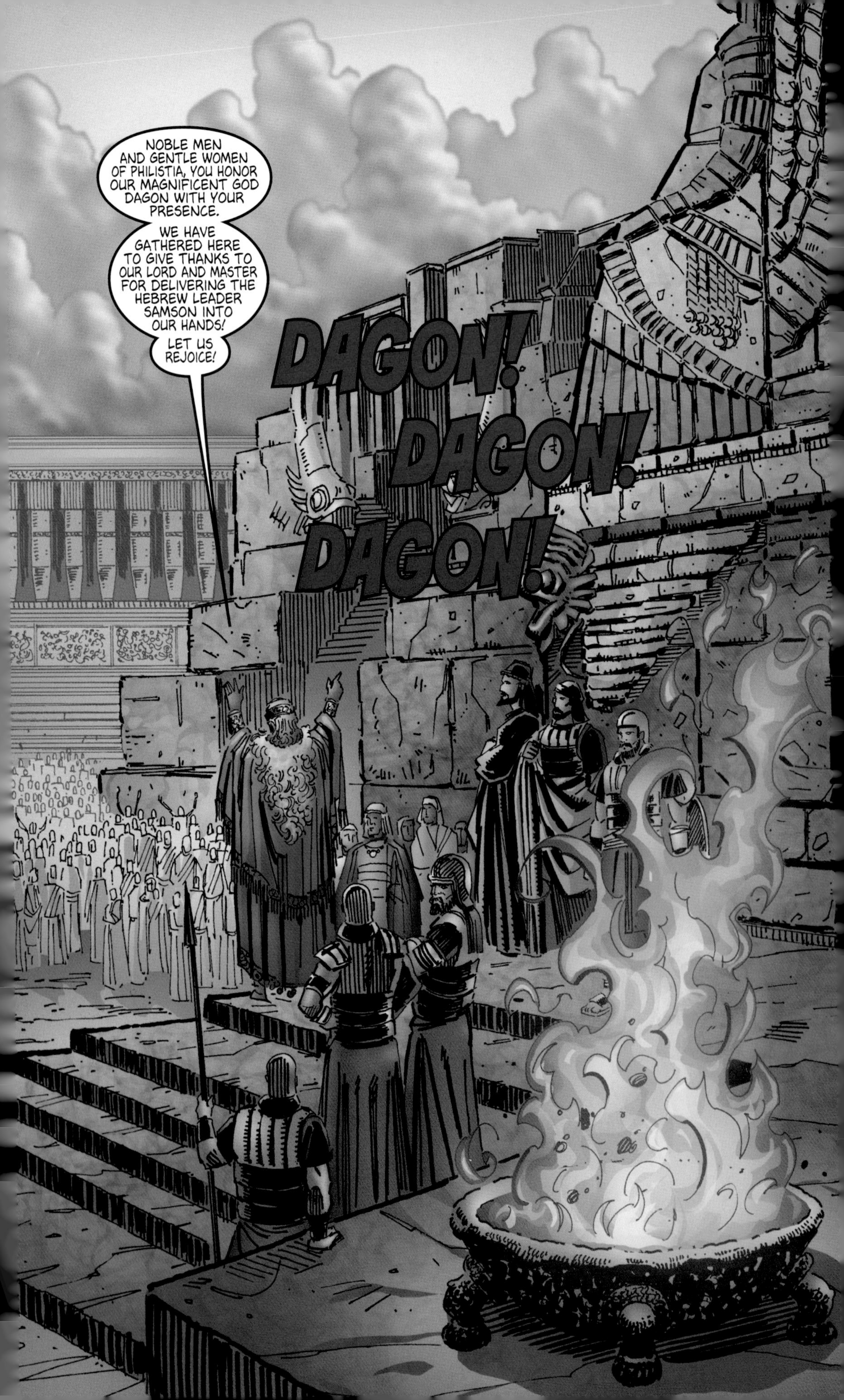
NOBLE MEN AND GENTLE WOMEN OF PHILISTIA, YOU HONOR OUR MAGNIFICENT GOD DAGON WITH YOUR PRESENCE.
WE HAVE GATHERED HERE TO GIVE THANKS TO OUR LORD AND MASTER FOR DELIVERING THE HEBREW LEADER SAMSON INTO OUR HANDS!
LET US REJOICE!
DAGON! DAGON! DAGON!

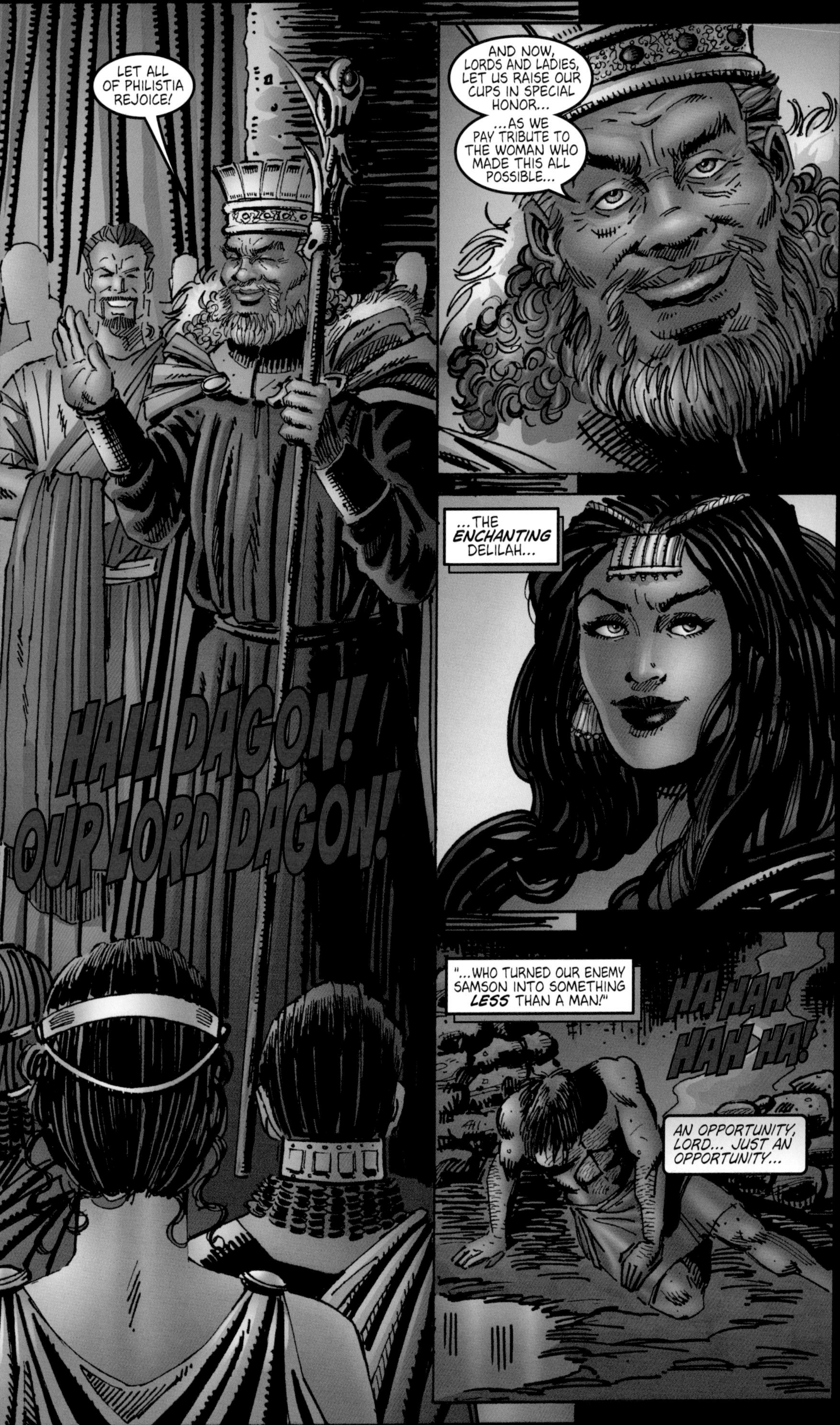
LET ALL OF PHILISTIA REJOICE!
HAIL DAGON! OUR LORD DAGON!
AND NOW, LORDS AND LADIES, LET US RAISE OUR CUPS IN SPECIAL HONOR...
...AS WE PAY TRIBUTE TO THE WOMAN WHO MADE THIS ALL POSSIBLE...
...THE *ENCHANTING* DELILAH...
"...WHO TURNED OUR ENEMY SAMSON INTO SOMETHING *LESS* THAN A MAN!"
HA HAH HAH HA!
AN OPPORTUNITY, LORD... JUST AN OPPORTUNITY...

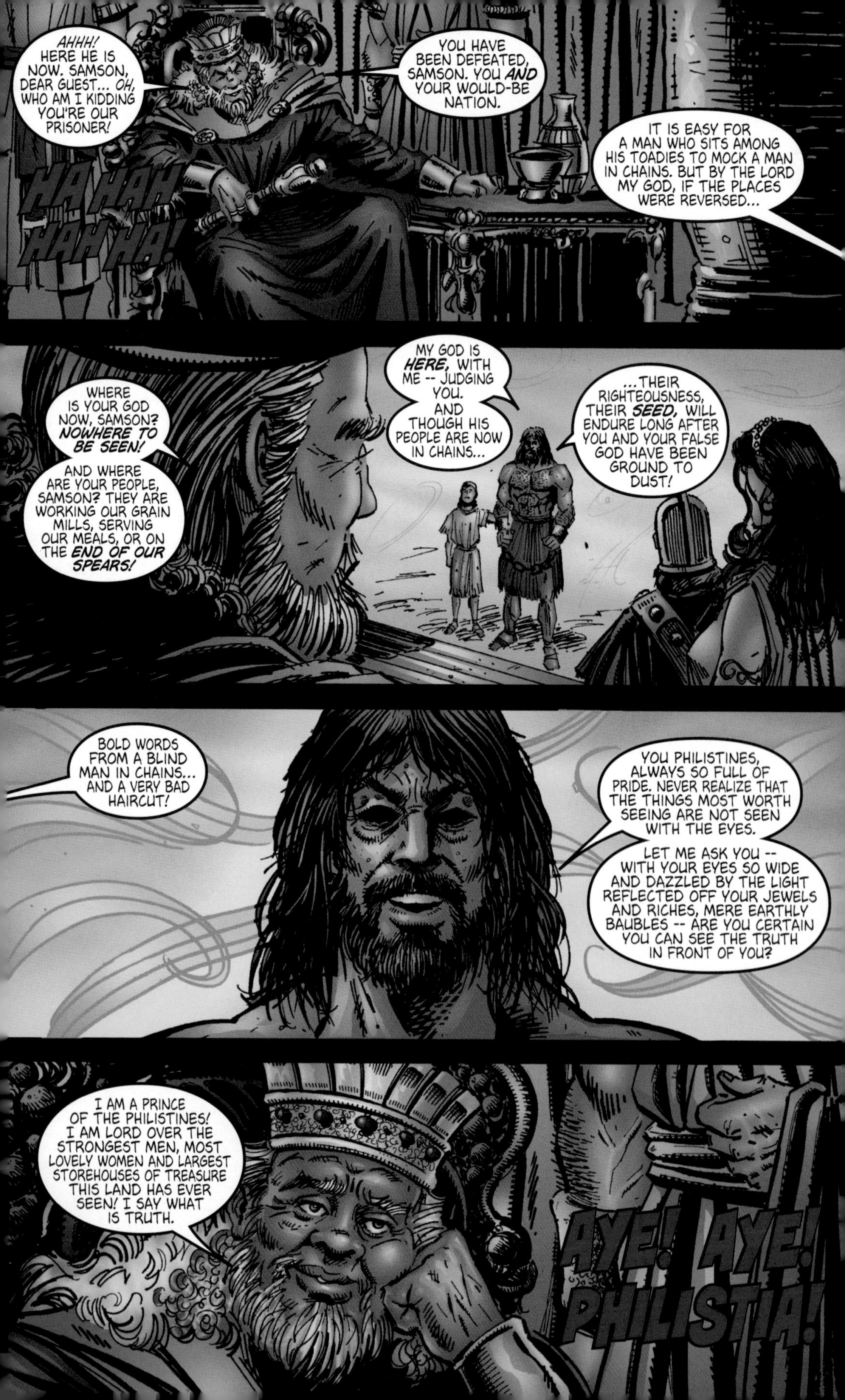

AHHH! HERE HE IS NOW. SAMSON, DEAR GUEST... OH, WHO AM I KIDDING YOU'RE OUR PRISONER!
YOU HAVE BEEN DEFEATED, SAMSON. YOU AND YOUR WOULD-BE NATION.
HA HAH HAH HA!
IT IS EASY FOR A MAN WHO SITS AMONG HIS TOADIES TO MOCK A MAN IN CHAINS. BUT BY THE LORD MY GOD, IF THE PLACES WERE REVERSED...
WHERE IS YOUR GOD NOW, SAMSON? NOWHERE TO BE SEEN!
AND WHERE ARE YOUR PEOPLE, SAMSON? THEY ARE WORKING OUR GRAIN MILLS, SERVING OUR MEALS, OR ON THE END OF OUR SPEARS!
MY GOD IS HERE, WITH ME -- JUDGING YOU. AND THOUGH HIS PEOPLE ARE NOW IN CHAINS...
...THEIR RIGHTEOUSNESS, THEIR SEED, WILL ENDURE LONG AFTER YOU AND YOUR FALSE GOD HAVE BEEN GROUND TO DUST!
BOLD WORDS FROM A BLIND MAN IN CHAINS... AND A VERY BAD HAIRCUT!
YOU PHILISTINES, ALWAYS SO FULL OF PRIDE. NEVER REALIZE THAT THE THINGS MOST WORTH SEEING ARE NOT SEEN WITH THE EYES.
LET ME ASK YOU -- WITH YOUR EYES SO WIDE AND DAZZLED BY THE LIGHT REFLECTED OFF YOUR JEWELS AND RICHES, MERE EARTHLY BAUBLES -- ARE YOU CERTAIN YOU CAN SEE THE TRUTH IN FRONT OF YOU?
I AM A PRINCE OF THE PHILISTINES! I AM LORD OVER THE STRONGEST MEN, MOST LOVELY WOMEN AND LARGEST STOREHOUSES OF TREASURE THIS LAND HAS EVER SEEN! I SAY WHAT IS TRUTH.
AYE! AYE! PHILISTIA!

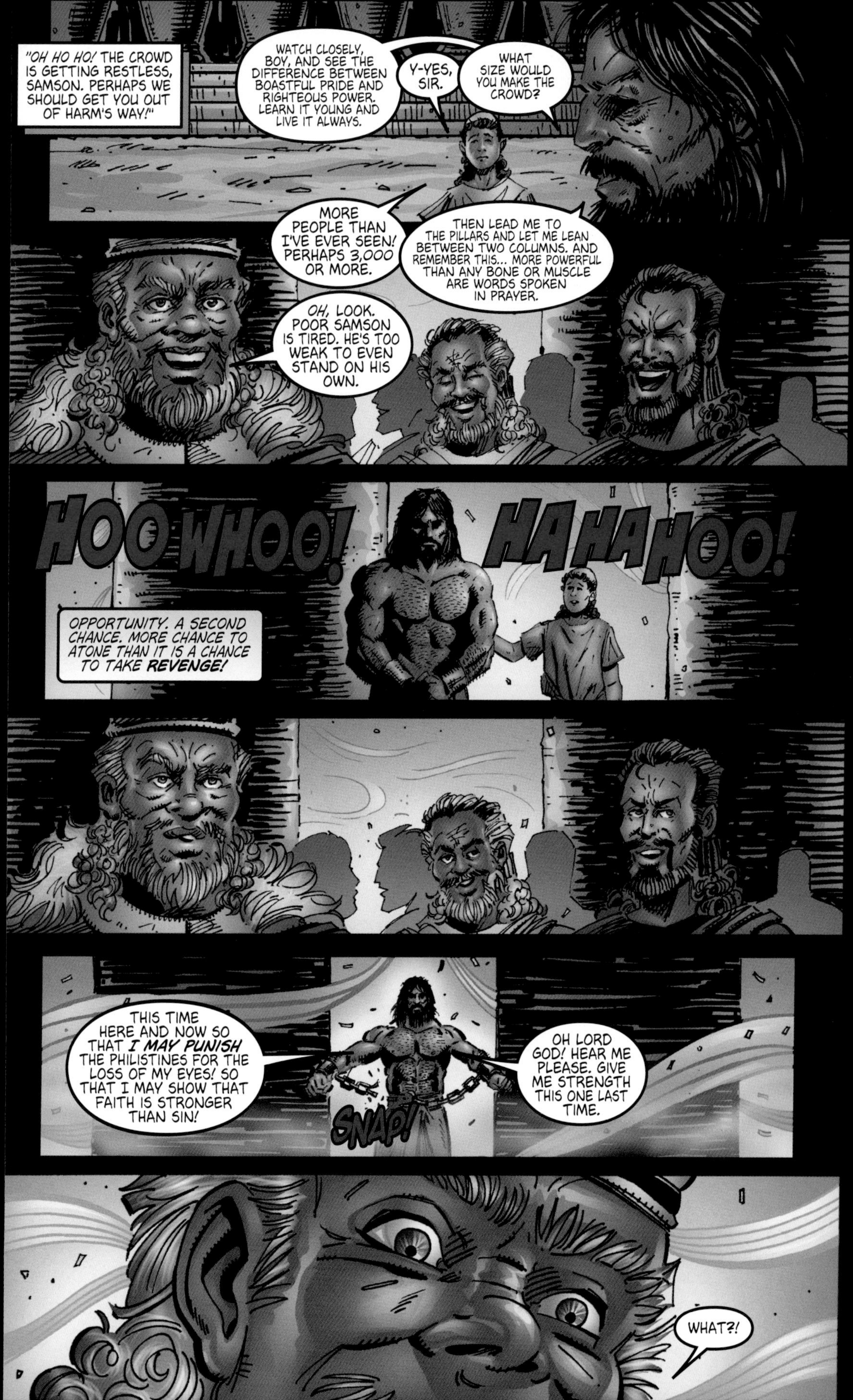
"OH HO HO! THE CROWD IS GETTING RESTLESS, SAMSON. PERHAPS WE SHOULD GET YOU OUT OF HARM'S WAY!"
WATCH CLOSELY, BOY, AND SEE THE DIFFERENCE BETWEEN BOASTFUL PRIDE AND RIGHTEOUS POWER. LEARN IT YOUNG AND LIVE IT ALWAYS.
Y-YES, SIR.
WHAT SIZE WOULD YOU MAKE THE CROWD?
MORE PEOPLE THAN I'VE EVER SEEN! PERHAPS 3,000 OR MORE.
THEN LEAD ME TO THE PILLARS AND LET ME LEAN BETWEEN TWO COLUMNS. AND REMEMBER THIS... MORE POWERFUL THAN ANY BONE OR MUSCLE ARE WORDS SPOKEN IN PRAYER.
OH, LOOK. POOR SAMSON IS TIRED. HE'S TOO WEAK TO EVEN STAND ON HIS OWN.
HOO WHOO!
HA HA HOO!
OPPORTUNITY. A SECOND CHANCE. MORE CHANCE TO ATONE THAN IT IS A CHANCE TO TAKE REVENGE!
OH LORD GOD! HEAR ME PLEASE. GIVE ME STRENGTH THIS ONE LAST TIME.
THIS TIME HERE AND NOW SO THAT I MAY PUNISH THE PHILISTINES FOR THE LOSS OF MY EYES! SO THAT I MAY SHOW THAT FAITH IS STRONGER THAN SIN!
SNAP!
WHAT?!

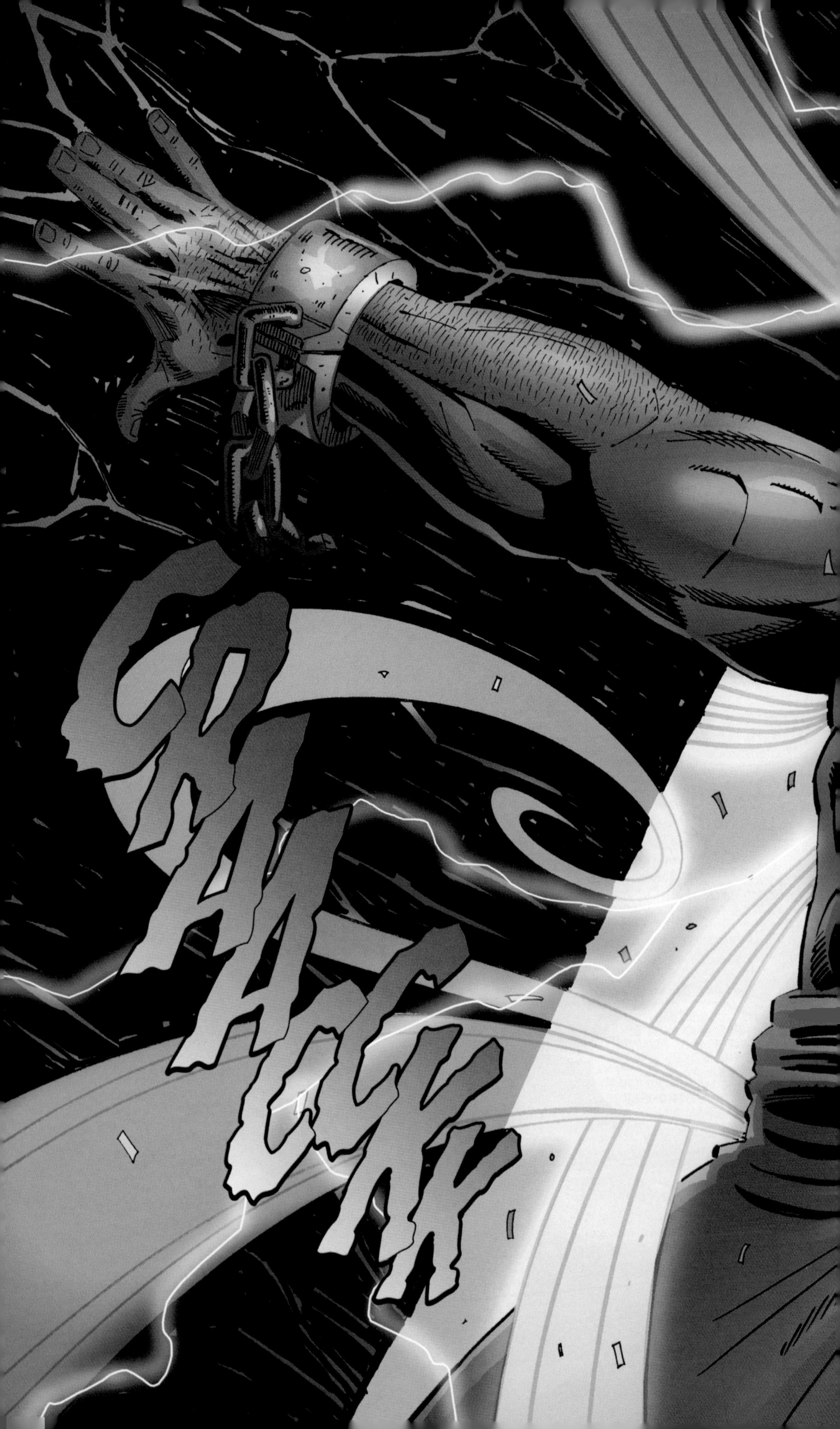
CRAACKK

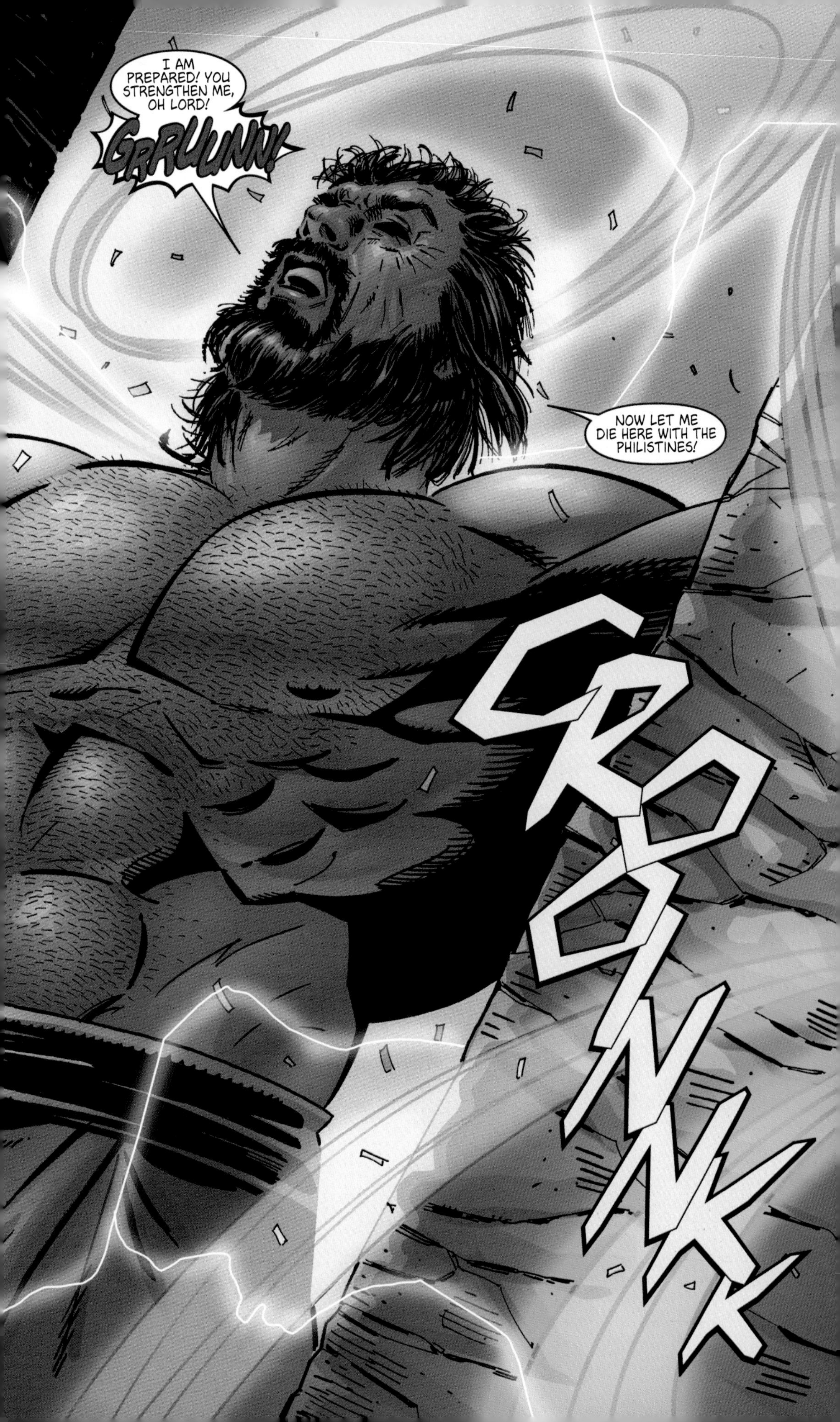
I AM PREPARED! YOU STRENGTHEN ME, OH LORD!
GRRUUNN!
NOW LET ME DIE HERE WITH THE PHILISTINES!
CRRINNKK

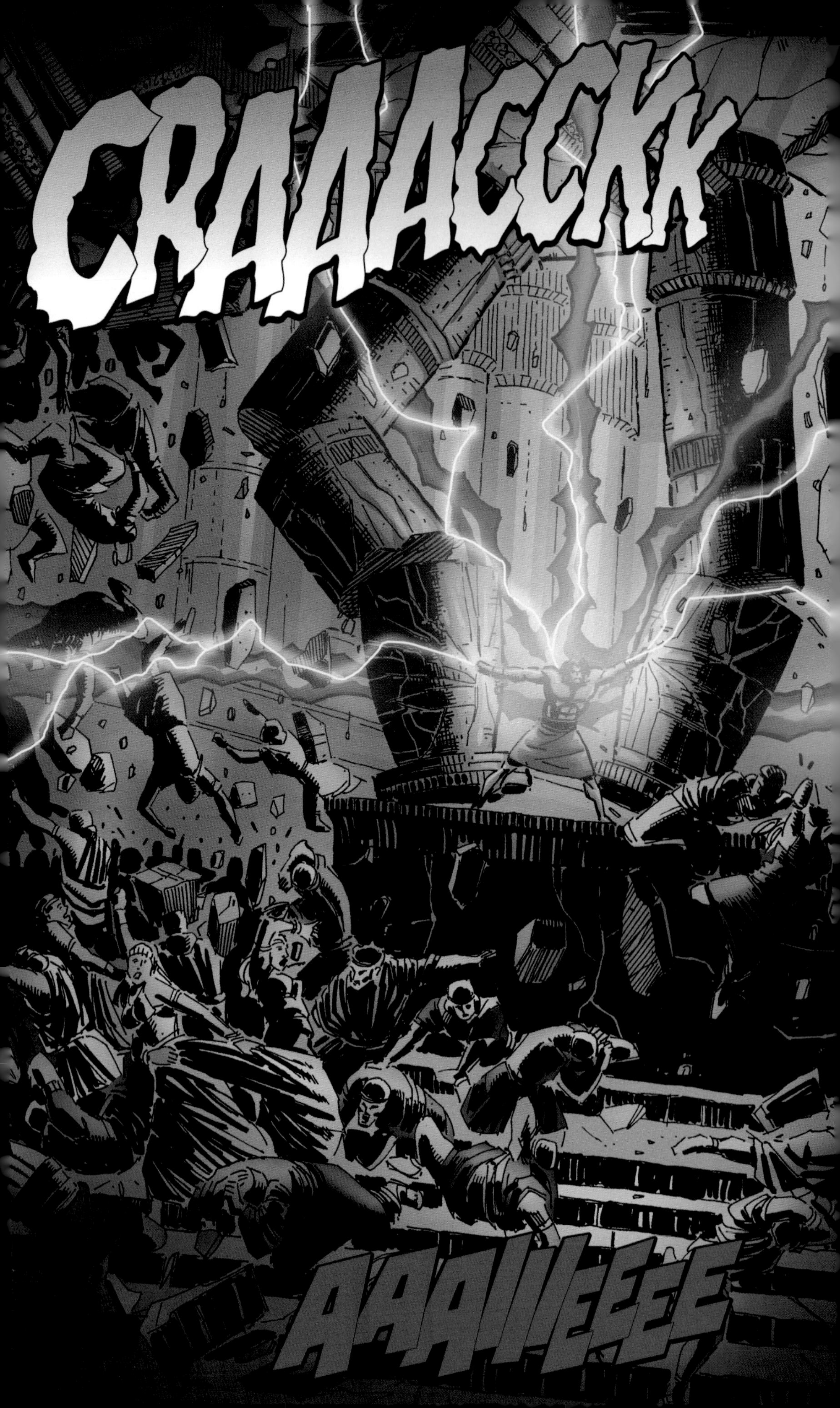
CRAAACCKK
AAAIIEEE

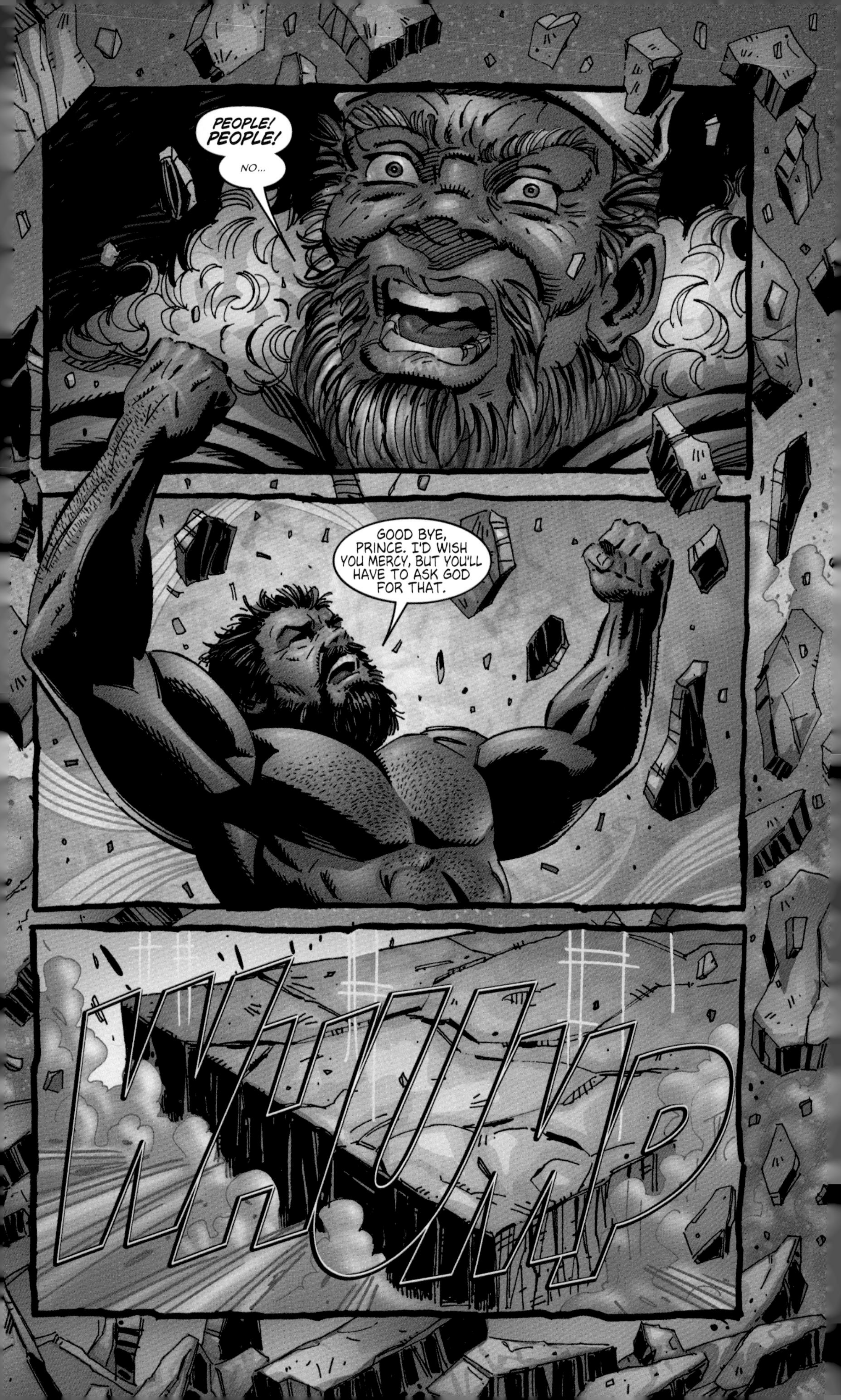
PEOPLE! PEOPLE!
NO...
GOOD BYE, PRINCE. I'D WISH YOU MERCY, BUT YOU'LL HAVE TO ASK GOD FOR THAT.
WHUMP

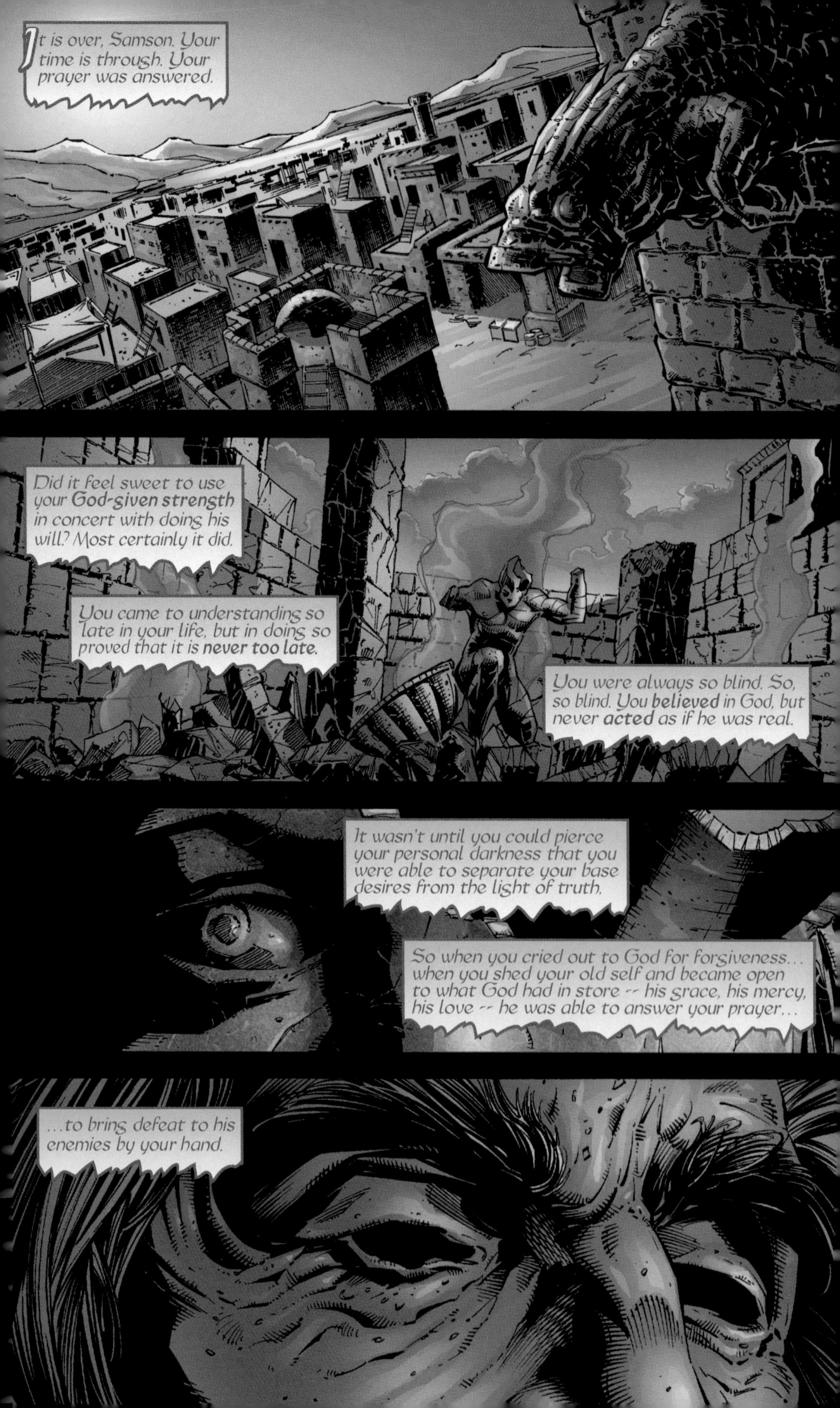
It is over, Samson. Your time is through. Your prayer was answered.
Did it feel sweet to use your **God-given strength** in concert with doing his will? Most certainly it did.
You came to understanding so late in your life, but in doing so proved that it is **never too late.**
You were always so blind. So, so blind. You **believed** in God, but never **acted** as if he was real.
It wasn't until you could pierce your personal darkness that you were able to separate your base desires from the light of truth.
So when you cried out to God for forgiveness... when you shed your old self and became open to what God had in store -- his grace, his mercy, his love -- he was able to answer your prayer...
...to bring defeat to his enemies by your hand.

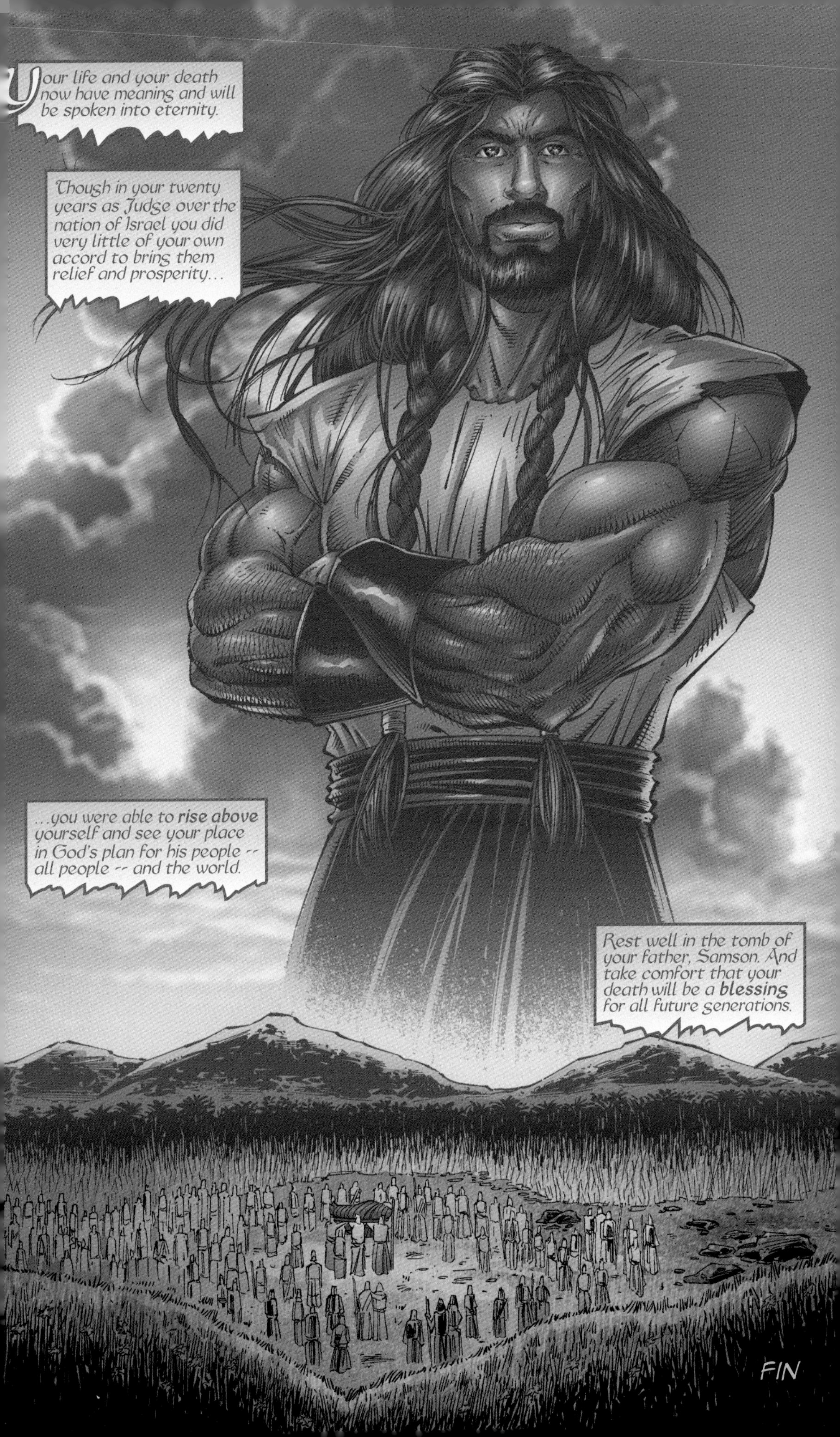
Your life and your death now have meaning and will be spoken into eternity.
Though in your twenty years as Judge over the nation of Israel you did very little of your own accord to bring them relief and prosperity...
...you were able to rise above yourself and see your place in God's plan for his people -- all people -- and the world.
Rest well in the tomb of your father, Samson. And take comfort that your death will be a blessing for all future generations.
FIN

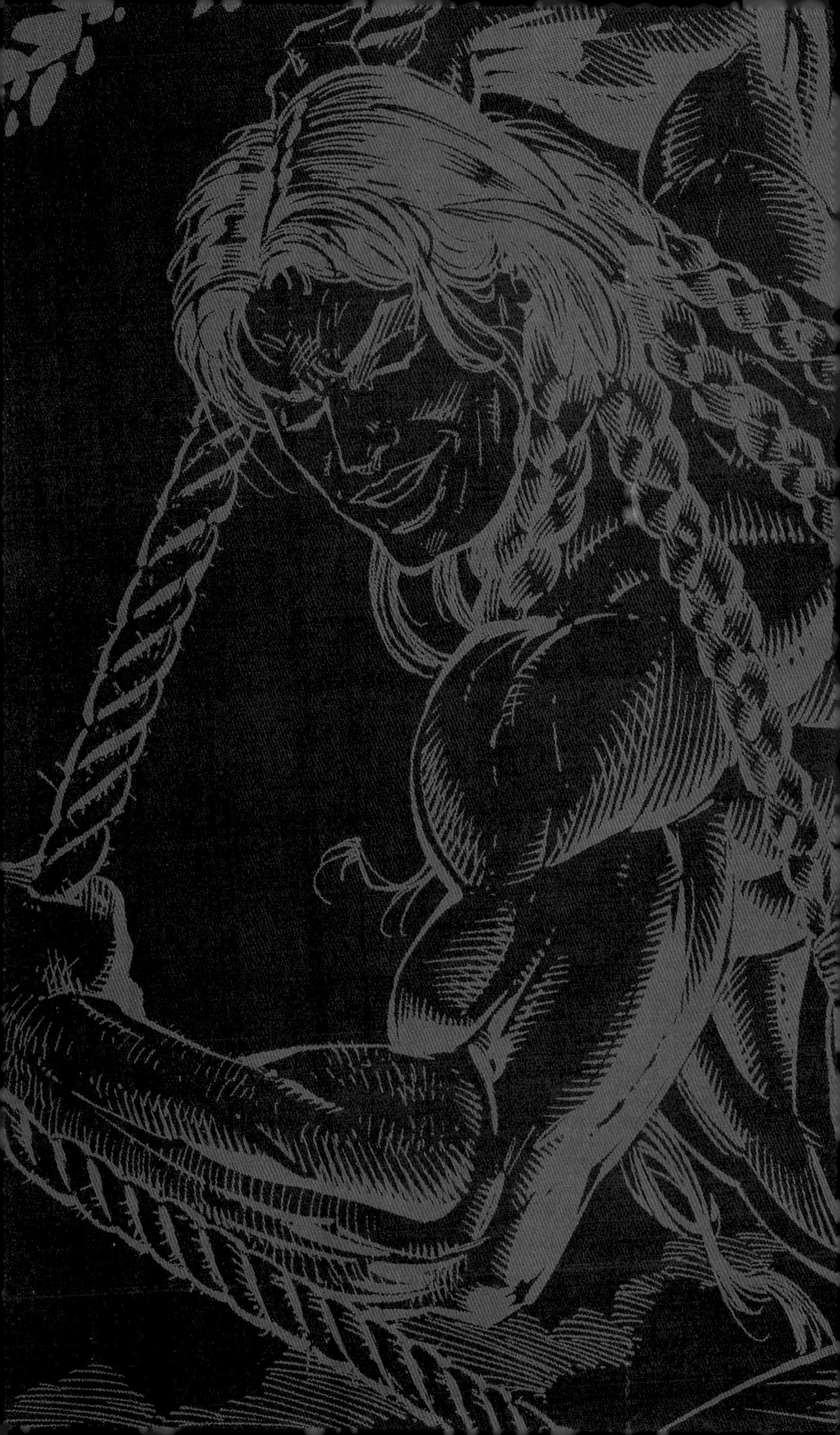

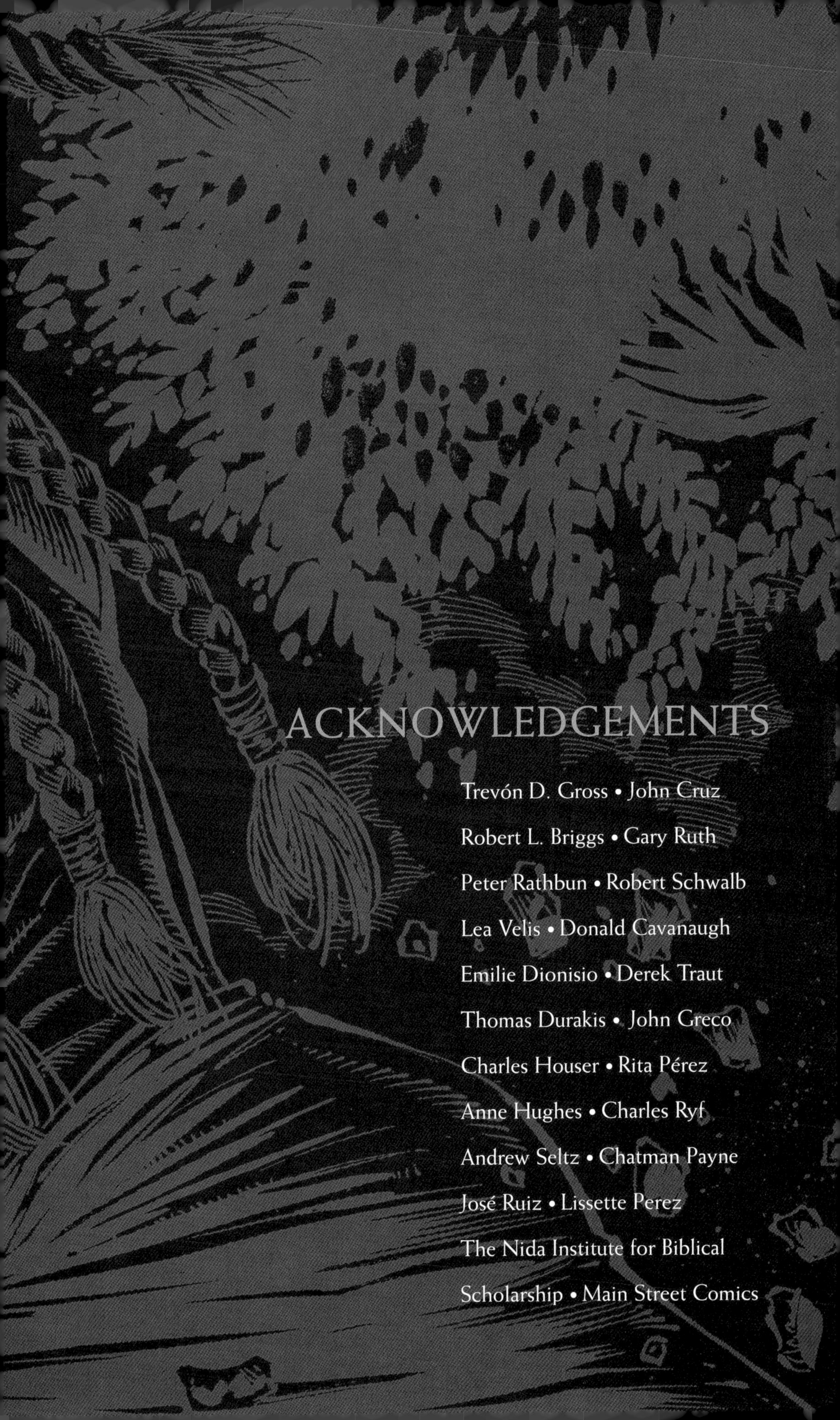

ACKNOWLEDGEMENTS

Trevón D. Gross • John Cruz

Robert L. Briggs • Gary Ruth

Peter Rathbun • Robert Schwalb

Lea Velis • Donald Cavanaugh

Emilie Dionisio • Derek Traut

Thomas Durakis • John Greco

Charles Houser • Rita Pérez

Anne Hughes • Charles Ryf

Andrew Seltz • Chatman Payne

José Ruiz • Lissette Perez

The Nida Institute for Biblical

Scholarship • Main Street Comics

Samson Is Born

13 Once again the Israelites started disobeying the LORD. So he let the Philistines take control of Israel for forty years.

²Manoah from the tribe of Dan lived in the town of Zorah. His wife was not able to have children, ³⁻⁵but one day an angel from the LORD appeared to her and said:

You have never been able to have any children, but very soon you will be pregnant and have a son. He will belong to God from the day he is born, so his hair must never be cut. And even before he is born, you must not drink any wine or beer or eat any food forbidden by God's laws.

Your son will begin to set Israel free from the Philistines.

⁶She went to Manoah and said, "A prophet who looked like an angel of God came and talked to me. I was so frightened, that I didn't even ask where he was from. He didn't tell me his name, ⁷but he did say that I'm going to have a baby boy. I'm not supposed to drink any wine or beer or eat any food forbidden by God's laws. Our son will belong to God for as long as he lives."

⁸Then Manoah prayed, "Our LORD, please send that prophet again and let him tell us what to do for the son we are going to have."

⁹God answered Manoah's prayer, and the angel went back to Manoah's wife while she was resting in the fields. Manoah wasn't there at the time, ¹⁰so she found him and said, "That same man is here again! He's the one I saw the other day."

¹¹Manoah went with his wife and asked the man, "Are you the one who spoke to my wife?"

"Yes, I am," he answered.

¹²Manoah then asked, "When your promise comes true, what rules must he obey and what will be his work?"

¹³"Your wife must be careful to do everything I told her," the LORD's angel answered. ¹⁴"She must not eat or drink anything made from grapes. She must not drink wine or beer or eat anything forbidden by God's laws. I told her exactly what to do."

¹⁵"Please," Manoah said, "stay here with us for just a little while, and we'll fix a young goat for you to eat." ¹⁶Manoah didn't realize that he was really talking to one of the LORD's angels.

The angel answered, "I can stay for a little while, although I won't eat any of your food. But if you would like to offer the goat as a sacrifice to the LORD, that would be fine."

¹⁷Manoah said, "Tell us your name, so we can honor you after our son is born."

¹⁸"No," the angel replied. "You don't need to know my name. And if you did, you couldn't understand it."

¹⁹So Manoah took a young goat over to a large rock he had chosen for an altar, and he built a fire on the rock. Then he killed the goat, and offered it with some grain as a sacrifice to the LORD. But then an amazing thing happened. ²⁰The fire blazed up toward the sky, and the LORD's angel went up toward heaven in the fire. Manoah and his wife bowed down low when they saw what happened.

²¹The angel was gone, but Manoah and his wife realized that he was one of the LORD's angels. ²²Manoah said, "We have seen an angel. Now we're going to die."

²³"The LORD isn't going to kill us," Manoah's wife responded. "The LORD accepted our sacrifice and grain offering, and he let us see something amazing. Besides, he told us that we're going to have a son."

²⁴Later, Manoah's wife did give birth to a son, and she named him Samson. As the boy grew, the LORD blessed him. ²⁵Then, while Samson was staying at Dan's Camp between the towns of Zorah and Eshtaol, the Spirit of the LORD took control of him.

Samson Gets Married

14 One day, Samson went to Timnah, where he saw a Philistine woman. ²When he got back home, he told his parents, "I saw a Philistine woman in Timnah, and I want to marry her. Get her for me!"

³His parents answered, "There are a lot of women in our clan and even more in the rest of Israel. Those Philistines are pagans. Why would you want to marry one of their women?"

"She looks good to me," Samson answered. "Get her for me!"

⁴At that time, the Philistines were in control of Israel, and the LORD wanted to stir up trouble for them. That's why he made Samson desire that woman.

⁵As Samson and his parents reached the vineyards near Timnah, a fierce young lion suddenly roared and attacked Samson. ⁶But the LORD's Spirit took control of Samson, and with his bare hands he tore the lion apart, as though it had been a young goat. His parents didn't know what he had done, and he didn't tell them.

⁷When they got to Timnah, Samson talked to the woman, and he was sure that she was the one for him.

⁸Later, Samson returned to Timnah for the wedding. And when he came near the place where the lion had attacked, he left the road to see what was left of the lion. He was surprised to see that bees were living in the lion's skeleton, and that they had made some honey. ⁹He scooped up the honey in his hands and ate some of it as he walked along. When he got back to his parents, he gave them some of the honey, and they ate it too. But he didn't tell them he had found the honey in the skeleton of a lion.

¹⁰While Samson's father went to make the final arrangements with the bride and her family, Samson threw a big party, as grooms usually did. ¹¹When the Philistines saw what Samson was like, they told thirty of their young men to stay with him at the party.

¹²Samson told the thirty young men, "This party will last for seven days. Let's make a bet: I'll tell you a riddle, and if you can tell me the right answer before the party is over, I'll give each one of you a shirt and a full change of clothing. ¹³But if you can't tell me the answer, then each of you will have to give me a shirt and a full change of clothing."

"It's a bet!" the Philistines said. "Tell us the riddle."

¹⁴Samson said:

Once so strong and mighty—
now so sweet and tasty!

Three days went by and the Philistine young men had not come up with the right answer. ¹⁵Finally, on the seventh day of the party they went to Samson's bride and said, "You had better trick your husband into telling you the answer to his riddle. Have you invited us here just to rob us? If you don't find out the answer, we will burn you and your family to death."

¹⁶Samson's bride went to him and started crying in his arms. "You must really hate me," she sobbed. "If you loved me at all, you would have told me the answer to your riddle."

"But I haven't even told my parents the answer!" Samson replied. "Why should I tell you?"

¹⁷For the entire seven days of the party, she had been whining and trying to get the answer from him. But that seventh day she put so much pressure on Samson that he finally gave in and told her the answer. She went straight to the young men and told them.

¹⁸Before sunset that day, the men of the town went to Samson with this answer:

A lion is the strongest—
honey is the sweetest!

Samson replied,

This answer you have given me doubtless came
from my bride-to-be.

¹⁹Then the LORD's Spirit took control of Samson. He went to Ashkelon, where he killed thirty men and took their clothing. Samson then gave it to the thirty young men at Timnah and stormed back home to his own family.

²⁰The father of the bride had Samson's wife marry one of the thirty young men that had been at Samson's party.

15 Later, during the wheat harvest, Samson went to visit the young woman he thought was still his wife.*ᵐ* He brought along a young goat as a gift and said to her father, "I want to go into my wife's bedroom."

"You can't do that," he replied. ²"When you left the way you did, I thought you were divorcing*ⁿ* her. So I arranged for her to marry one of the young men who were at your party. But my younger daughter is even prettier, and you can have her as your wife."

³"This time," Samson answered, "I have a good reason for really hurting some Philistines."

Samson Takes Revenge

⁴Samson went out and caught three hundred foxes and tied them together in pairs with oil-soaked rags around their tails. ⁵Then Samson took the foxes into the Philistine wheat fields that were ready to be harvested. He set the rags on fire and let the foxes go. The wheat fields went up in flames, and so did the stacks of wheat that had already been cut. Even the Philistine vineyards and olive orchards burned.

⁶Some of the Philistines started asking around, "Who could have done such a thing?"

"It was Samson," someone told them. "He married the daughter of that man in Timnah, but then the man gave Samson's wife to one of the men at the wedding."

The Philistine leaders went to Timnah and burned to death Samson's wife and her father.

⁷When Samson found out what they had done, he went to them and said, "You killed them! And I won't rest until I get even with you." ⁸Then Samson started hacking them to pieces with his sword.

Samson left Philistia and went to live in the cave at Etam Rock. ⁹But it wasn't long before the Philistines invaded Judah and set up a huge army camp at Jawbone.

¹⁰The people of Judah asked, "Why have you invaded our land?"

The Philistines answered, "We've come to get Samson. We're going to do the same things to him that he did to our people."

¹¹Three thousand men from Judah went to the cave at Etam Rock and said to Samson, "Don't you know that the Philistines rule us, and they will punish us for what you did?"

"I was only getting even with them," Samson replied. "They did the same things to me first."

¹²"We came here to tie you up and turn you over to them," said the men of Judah.

"I won't put up a fight," Samson answered, "but you have to promise not to hurt me yourselves."

¹³⁻¹⁴"We promise," the men said. "We will only tie you up and turn you over to the Philistines. We won't kill you." Then they tied up his hands and arms with two brand-new ropes and led him away from Etam Rock.

When the Philistines saw that Samson was being brought to their camp at Jawbone, they started shouting and ran toward him. But the LORD's Spirit took control of Samson, and Samson broke the ropes, as though they were pieces of burnt cloth. ¹⁵Samson glanced around and spotted the jawbone of a donkey. The jawbone had not yet dried out, so it was still hard and heavy. Samson grabbed it and started hitting Philistines—he killed a thousand of them! ¹⁶After the fighting was over, he made up this poem about what he had done to the Philistines:

> I used a donkey's jawbone
>   to kill a thousand men;
> I beat them with this jawbone
>   over and over again.

¹⁷Samson tossed the jawbone on the ground and decided to call the place Jawbone Hill. It is still called that today.

¹⁸Samson was so thirsty that he prayed, "Our LORD, you helped me win a battle against a whole army. Please don't let me die of thirst now. Those heathen Philistines will carry off my dead body."

¹⁹Samson was tired and weary, but God sent water gushing from a rock. Samson drank some and felt strong again.

Samson named the place Caller Spring, because he had called out to God for help. The spring is still there at Jawbone.

²⁰Samson was a leader of Israel for twenty years, but the Philistines were still the rulers of Israel.

Samson Carries Off the Gates of Gaza

16 One day while Samson was in Gaza, he saw a prostitute and went to her house to spend the night. ²The people who lived in Gaza found out he was there, and they decided to kill him at sunrise. So they went to the city gate and waited all night in the guardrooms on each side of the gate.

³But Samson got up in the middle of the night and went to the town gate. He pulled the gate doors and doorposts out of the wall and put them on his shoulders. Then he carried them all the way to the top of the hill that overlooks Hebron, where he set the doors down, still closed and locked.

Delilah Tricks Samson

⁴Some time later, Samson fell in love with a woman named Delilah, who lived in Sorek Valley. ⁵The Philistine rulers went to Delilah and said, "Trick Samson into telling you what makes him so strong and what can make him weak. Then we can tie him up so he can't get away. If you find out his secret, we will each give you eleven hundred pieces of silver."

⁶The next time Samson was at Delilah's house, she asked, "Samson, what makes you so strong? How can I tie you up so you can't get away? Come on, you can tell me."

⁷Samson answered, "If someone ties me up with seven new bowstrings that have never been dried, it will make me just as weak as anyone else."

⁸⁻⁹The Philistine rulers gave seven new bowstrings to Delilah. They also told some of their soldiers to go to Delilah's house and hide in the room where Samson and Delilah were. If the bowstrings made Samson weak, they would be able to capture him.

Delilah tied up Samson with the bowstrings and shouted, "Samson, the Philistines are attacking!"

Samson snapped the bowstrings, as though they were pieces of scorched string. The Philistines had not found out why Samson was so strong.

¹⁰"You lied and made me look like a fool," Delilah said. "Now tell me. How can I really tie you up?"

¹¹Samson answered, "Use some new ropes. If I'm tied up with ropes that have never been used, I'll be just as weak as anyone else."

¹²Delilah got new ropes and again had some Philistines hide in the room. Then she tied up Samson's arms and shouted, "Samson, the Philistines are attacking!"

Samson snapped the ropes as if they were threads.

¹³"You're still lying and making a fool of me," Delilah said. "Tell me how I can tie you up!"

"My hair is in seven braids," Samson replied. "If you weave my braids into the threads on a loom and nail the loom to a wall, then I will be as weak as anyone else."

¹⁴While Samson was asleep, Delilah wove his braids into the threads on a loom and nailed the loom to a wall. Then she shouted, "Samson, the Philistines are attacking!"

Samson woke up and pulled the loom free from its posts in the ground and from the nails in the wall. Then he pulled his hair free from the woven cloth.

¹⁵"Samson," Delilah said, "you claim to love me, but you don't mean it! You've made me look like a fool three times now, and you still haven't told me why you are so strong." ¹⁶Delilah started nagging and pestering him day after day, until he couldn't stand it any longer.

¹⁷Finally, Samson told her the truth. "I have belonged to God ever since I was born, so my hair has never been cut. If it were ever cut off, my strength would leave me, and I would be as weak as anyone else."

¹⁸Delilah realized that he was telling the truth. So she sent someone to tell the Philistine rulers, "Come to my house one more time. Samson has finally told me the truth."

The Philistine rulers went to Delilah's house, and they brought along the silver they had promised her. ¹⁹Delilah had lulled Samson to sleep with his head resting in her lap. She signalled to one of the Philistine men as she began cutting off Samson's seven braids. And by the time she was finished, Samson's strength was gone. Delilah tied him up ²⁰and shouted, "Samson, the Philistines are attacking!"

Samson woke up and thought, "I'll break loose and escape, just as I always do." He did not realize that the LORD had stopped helping him.

21The Philistines grabbed Samson and poked out his eyes. They took him to the prison in Gaza and chained him up. Then they put him to work, turning a millstone to grind grain. **22**But they didn't cut his hair any more, so it started growing back.

23The Philistine rulers threw a big party and sacrificed a lot of animals to their god Dagon. The rulers said:

> Samson was our enemy,
> but our god Dagon
>   helped us capture him!

24-25 Everyone there was having a good time, and they shouted, "Bring out Samson—he's still good for a few more laughs!"

The rulers had Samson brought from the prison, and when the people saw him, this is how they praised their god:

> Samson ruined our crops
>   and killed our people.
> He was our enemy,
> but our god helped us
>   capture him.

They made fun of Samson for a while, then they told him to stand near the columns that supported the roof. **26**A young man was leading Samson by the hand, and Samson said to him, "I need to lean against something. Take me over to the columns that hold up the roof."

27The Philistine rulers were celebrating in a temple packed with people and with three thousand more on the flat roof. They had all been watching Samson and making fun of him.

28Samson prayed, "Please remember me, Lord God. The Philistines poked out my eyes, but make me strong one last time, so I can take revenge for at least one of my eyes!"

29Samson was standing between the two middle columns that held up the roof. He felt around and found one column with his right hand, and the other with his left hand. **30**Then he shouted, "Let me die with the Philistines!" He pushed against the columns as hard as he could, and the temple collapsed with the Philistine rulers and everyone else still inside. Samson killed more Philistines when he died than he had killed during his entire life.

31His brothers and the rest of his family went to Gaza and took his body back home. They buried him in his father's tomb, which was located between Zorah and Eshtaol.

Samson was a leader of Israel for twenty years.

THE W·ORD
C·E·V